Ideas for Canvas Work

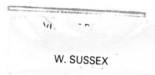
VIANF

Ideas for Canvas Work

Mary Rhodes

B. T. Batsford Limited, London

© Mary Rhodes 1970

First published 1970

Second impression 1971

First paperback edition 1984

ISBN 0 7134 4613 7

Cover illustration: Detail from *Radiating Circles*.
A most attractive textural effect has been created
by a discriminate use of stitches. It is worked with
Appleton wools and raffene in bright and cheerful
colours. *Shirley Windle*

Printed in Great Britain by
The Anchor Press, Tiptree, Essex
for the publishers
B. T. Batsford Limited
4 Fitzhardinge Street, London W1H 0AH

Contents

Acknowledgment

I should like to thank Miss Dorothy Allsopp and Miss Iris Hills of the ILEA Inspectorate, Mrs Ivy Cooper-Marsh, Principal of Eltham Adult Institute and most particularly Miss Margaret Peel Yates, Principal of Greenwich Adult Institute, for all their help and encouragement in my work as a tutor for Tapestry and Embroidery, which has led through the cheerful efforts of my students over many happy years to the production of this book.

All the pieces of work photographed, with the exception of a few by myself, have been produced by my students at Greenwich and Eltham ILEA Adult Institutes, and without their great help and interest this book could not have been written. Many of the photographs show details of larger pieces of work, and in some cases these are first efforts. I should like, therefore, to thank here all my students, past and present, who have so kindly allowed me to have their work photographed for use in the text.

My thanks are also due to Miss Constance Howard, Head of the Department of Embroidery and Textiles at Goldsmiths College, for the inspiration of her classes and for her kind suggestion that I should approach with my ideas on canvas work Miss Thelma M. Nye of B. T. Batsford Limited, to whom I am also greatly indebted for giving the work its proper direction and always being ready with most helpful comments and suggestions.

In addition, I should like to thank Miss Julie Dorrington for permitting me to use one of her photographs in figure 82, Mr John Minshall for his skilful photographing of the mirror with the surround of cubes, figure 263, and Mr John Hunnex for the four excellent colour plates. For the bulk of the photography, however, and the typing of the manuscript, as well as for his assistance with the proofs, I have to thank my husband, whose constant help and encouragement in all ways have made it possible for me to write this book.

Eltham 1970   M.R.

Introduction

Canvas embroidery has been produced in England ever since the Tudor period, but it has tended in modern times to move away from the fine and intricate designs of earlier days, which depended on a skilful blending of various stitches, with tent stitch being used to preserve the finer lines of the design, towards a rather heavy and formless interpretation of design, which appears to have occurred as a result of allowing the nature of the canvas background to restrict too strongly the mode of expression. The prevalent use of certain square stitches, which have been held to be those most suitable for working on canvas, has led to designs being interpreted in a rigid, angular manner. Whilst agreeing with those who think that designs should be suited to the nature and special characteristics of the medium in which one is working, I nevertheless feel that this rigid and angular interpretation is not the only satisfactory way of working on canvas, and I shall, therefore, attempt to show in the following pages a different and, for me at least, more satisfying approach to this subject, and one which I feel is more in keeping with the idiom of today. It is my intention not only to show what is to my mind a livelier method of interpreting designs on to canvas whilst using the more conventional stitches and materials, but also to indicate what can be done in this medium by the introduction of more unusual materials, including various types of 'found' object, and by modifying the canvas background itself by cutting shapes into it and thus allowing a chosen further background to show through.

1 The position of canvas work in modern embroidery

In most exhibitions of embroidery at the present time, canvas work tends to be accorded very little space, and this may well be the result of the fact that many exponents of this branch of the embroiderer's craft have mistakenly allowed themselves to be restricted too closely by what they consider to be the exigencies of their medium. Their seeming obsession with the form of the basic material on which they work has resulted in the production of examples of canvas embroidery in which designs have been executed in a heavy and very pedestrian manner, and which have in consequence little appeal for a world grown accustomed to a much freer and more vigorous and lively interpretation of ideas.

The best examples of canvas embroidery in the time of its highest achievement in the period from the late sixteenth to the eighteenth century show a clarity of line and a faithfulness in the interpretation of design which have largely been lost in the modern predilection for 'square' stitches and its accompanying rejection of the use of tent stitch. The fact that the art of canvas embroidery declined in the nineteenth century and the early years of the twentieth century, and that uninspired pieces of work were produced in which tent stitch was often used to make slavish copies in silk and wool of floral paintings, landscapes and portraits, has led some modern designers to reject tent stitch out of hand, because they think it will always produce a monotonous result and be a restraining influence in the development of lively, modern pieces of work. This is in my opinion a great mistake, which has itself exerted the same kind of restricting influence on the true development of the craft as that which it was intended to combat. Tent stitch remains, I believe, a vital necessity in the working of designs for small pieces which will be subjected to close scrutiny and particularly for the interpretation of linear designs, which are otherwise completely lost in the finished work. If the outline of a linear design is first worked in tent stitch, it is then possible freely to employ 'square' stitches, either for the background or for other large areas of the design, with further use of tent stitch to fill any gaps between the square stitches and the tent-stitch outline, and, by thus keeping the perfect outline of the original drawing, all suggestion of 'stepping', which is such a typical and, to my mind, unattractive feature of many modern pieces of canvas embroidery, can be avoided.

A further feature of recent modern practice in canvas embroidery is the employment of a variety of stitches, producing a corresponding variety of texture, often apparently for the sake of variety and not for the sake of the design. This practice leads to particularly grotesque results when natural forms are used in a design and are then interpreted by the quite arbitrary use of a range of stitches to give an 'interesting' juxtaposition of textures without regard at all to the natural form which the work seeks to depict. In making this assertion I do not in the least suggest that one should aim at a rigidly naturalistic interpretation of designs based on forms taken from Nature, but I do maintain that one should regard the great variety of stitches available to the canvas embroiderer as offering an opportunity to choose those which can best convey some textural quality of the natural object which is being depicted. Even when one is working abstract designs on to canvas, it is necessary to observe carefully the effect which is likely to be created by a change of stitch, with its accompanying change in texture, as otherwise the balance and unity of a design can easily be destroyed.

1   Detail of cushion worked on 16-mesh canvas in silk and wool. The colouring is black, white and blue-green on a background of cushion stitch in crimson

Elsie Smout

2   Chair seat. One of a set of six worked in tent stitch. This design still shows the traditional way of shading flowers, but the background is beginning to show signs of change, not only in the treatment of shading but also in the colour scheme which is black, silver-grey and rose-red   *Majorie Chalk*

3   This small panel shows the successful use of tent stitch to interpret a linear design rich in bold sweeping curves   *May Thurgood*

◀ 4   Tent stitch picture size 15 in. × 20 in. on 16 mesh. Worked mainly in blues, greens, yellow and white. An attempt to show movement and light   *Betty Wyatt*

5   Stool top. Tent stitch on 9/18 Penelope canvas. The double threads of this canvas were split to work this stool top, so making it 18 threads to the inch. It is difficult to split the threads of this canvas and, if possible, single-thread canvas should always be used
   Rennie Westmacott

6   This rhinoceros would probably have been more successful if the stitches had been allowed to follow the natural contours of the body and it had not been treated as an area to be filled with random stitches   *Lilian Hill*

7 Detail of a floral panel on 16-mesh canvas. Tent stitch with a blue background. This shows clearly the method of shading. The sunflower is very simply treated. It has a yellow silk outline around each petal, the remaining area of the petals are shaded with single lines of five shades of colour ranging from buttercup yellow through orange to brown centre veins *Rösli Warren*

8   *Blue Flower*. Using a white or light-coloured silk for outlining half of the petal with the other half in very dark blue wool and the intermediate shades in between, enables this blue flower to stand out boldly on its self-coloured background.

Rösli Warren

Opposite

9 Two lively horses worked entirely in tent stitch. No attempt has been made in any way to treat the horses in a naturalistic manner. A variety of stitches has been used for the background   *Terese Blackall*

10 Details of a panel, showing the moving away from the traditional shading of leaves to a much freer and simpler treatment   *Gladys Barry*

11 *Sunrise*. Small picture in pinks, yellows and purple. A stylised treatment of a bird on a pale yellow background. Wool, silk and nylon raffia were used for the various stitches which include double-knot stitch   *Miriam Bawden*

2   Designing for canvas embroidery

When embarking on a design for canvas embroidery, one must, of course, first have clearly in mind the purpose for which the finished piece of work is to be used, whether it is to serve some practical purpose, as, for instance, a cover for a chair seat or a cushion, or is to be put to a purely decorative purpose, such as a wallhanging, picture or mirror surround. If something practical is decided on, then naturally a design has to be prepared which is suitable for working with materials which are strong and durable, and it will be limited by this fact in a way that a design for a purely decorative object need not be. It is also necessary at this stage to recognise clearly that great thought and care should be given, not only to the design and its suitability for the purpose envisaged, but also to the nature of the materials to be used and the method of working, as, with care and good fortune, a piece of canvas work could well be preserved for centuries, and we should be concerned to bequeath to future generations something that will be both aesthetically satisfying as regards its design, and also capable of preserving its original beauty as nearly as possible unimpaired by the passage of time.

For practical purposes

In preparing designs for practical objects, the factor mainly to be borne in mind at the start is the type of stitch to be used. Naturally only the strongest stitches should be employed, and of these the most important, as also the most durable, is tent stitch, often referred to as petit point. This does not mean that all furniture covers should be worked solely in that stitch, as certain square stitches are also suitable and can be used in conjunction with tent stitch, according to the nature of the design. If it is decided to use only tent stitch in the working, then the design must be drawn with the fact in mind that tent stitch is a linear stitch and is, therefore, unsuitable for working large areas of unbroken colour. If such areas of unbroken colour are felt to be essential to a design, then some type of square stitch should be employed to give character to these areas of colour by means of its varied texture. It follows, however, that a square stitch by its very nature is unsuitable for using exclusively to interpret linear designs, where curves abound, for, if this is done, it results in a complete loss of the original line of the design and produces a clumsy and formless effect, which lacks any real character. What is, in fact, essential in all good design applies especially here, that the designer must always have clearly in mind the nature and special limiting features of the materials to be used, so that he or she does not demand from the medium something which it cannot adequately offer, and does not neglect to exploit fully certain attributes which the medium possesses to a special degree.

For decorative purposes

When it comes to preparing designs for a picture or wall-panel in canvas work, a very free treatment can be employed. Present-day pop and abstract art have led to a complete relaxation of rules as far as the artist is concerned, and this tendency is noticeable also in embroidery. Many different types of material can be used; the whole surface of the canvas does not necessarily require to be covered with stitchery; the canvas may have an irregular shape, and holes may be cut into it; and a wide variety of found objects, such as glass, stones, bark, shells or pieces of metal can be incorporated in conjunction with various canvas embroidery stitches in the worked parts. A great deal of latitude is permissible, and this can lead to much fun and enjoyment in the working-out of suitable designs to accommodate the wide range of materials it is possible to use.

Source of designs

The actual preparation of designs for canvas work presents to most people, who have not been specially trained for it, the greatest difficulty, and many will not even attempt it. I would, however, appeal to such persons not to give up the attempt entirely, as it is perfectly possible for them to try methods other than the conventional one of drawing with pencil on paper. After many years experience of teaching canvas embroidery, I have come to the conclusion that in fact only those who are capable of forming a reasonably clear mental image in colour of the finished work at the time they begin to draw should attempt to produce a design straight away with pencil and paper. Others will need to adopt a method of procedure which will enable them to discover a suitable arrangement of shapes in colour that seems likely to lead to a satisfactory design for the purpose they envisage. Design, after all, simply means good arrangement and the creation of order out of chaos.

Among such other methods of producing attractive and workable designs for canvas embroidery is that of cutting out paper shapes and moving them around on a table, either on a sheet of paper or on the actual canvas to be used, within the outline shape it is wished to fill, until a result which is pleasing to the eye is finally obtained. Thin tissue paper is useful for this purpose, as the paper shapes can then be overlapped and the overlapping will add a suggestion of tone, which can itself be helpful when it comes to working out the final colour scheme. In order to achieve greater originality in producing a design by this method, and to avoid one's own predisposition to arrange the shapes in certain, perhaps limited, ways, it may sometimes be a good idea in the first instance to drop the cut-out paper shapes at random on to the sheet of paper or canvas and then to make adjustments to them so as to obtain balance in the design by removing some shapes or by separating them from one another and thus allowing interesting areas of background to show through. When a satisfactory arrangement of the chosen shapes is arrived at, the method of proceeding is as follows: if the paper shapes have been arranged upon a paper background, a sheet of tracing paper or greaseproof paper should be placed over the whole design and the outline of the shape should be traced; if, on the other hand, the shapes have been arranged upon the actual canvas, their outline should be drawn directly on to the canvas by means of a brush and black paint. The design thus obtained will provide a basis upon which further connecting lines may be drawn between the original shapes to give unity to the whole.

Cutting or tearing simple shapes out of a strip, circle or square of paper, that has first been folded, is another way of discovering useful ideas for a design. The paper can be folded in a variety of ways, can then be opened out and cut down the centre, so that the two halves may be moved independently of one another, or can be further embellished by cutting.

12　Cut paper shapes. With a carefully chosen colour scheme and stitches this design lends itself excellently to canvas work

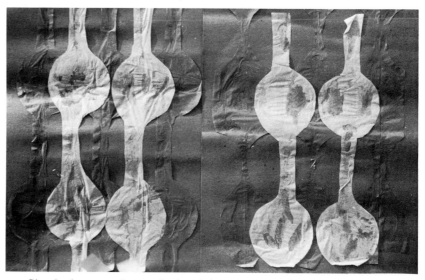

13　Simple shapes cut in two shades of tissue paper overlapped

14 Detail of small picture adapted from a Christmas card. This could have been
designed by the cut-paper method   *Sheila Gibson*

15 Torn paper gives interesting results quite different from cutting

16 Cut paper. Slightly altered this could form a basis for a suitable design for working on canvas

17 Torn thin card which automatically curves will give shapes which can be interpreted differently from the shapes cut or torn in paper

18 *Christmas Balls.* This design was based on overlapping paper shapes *Geraldine Self*

19 *Nürnberg.* Detail of panel. Designed with the aid of a ruler and set square *Rose Cussens*

20 Triangles and circles. Cut-paper design, worked with coton-à-broder, wool, silk, wooden and glass beads and canvas threads

Winifred Jury

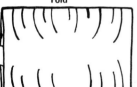

Fold

Fold

Cut a 6 in. square of paper. Fold and cut a few lines from the folded side

Fold

21 A 6 in. square of paper folded and cut, together with a sketch showing the development of the design

22 Similar to 21

23   Cardboard rim of a cheese carton

24   Sketches suggested by 23

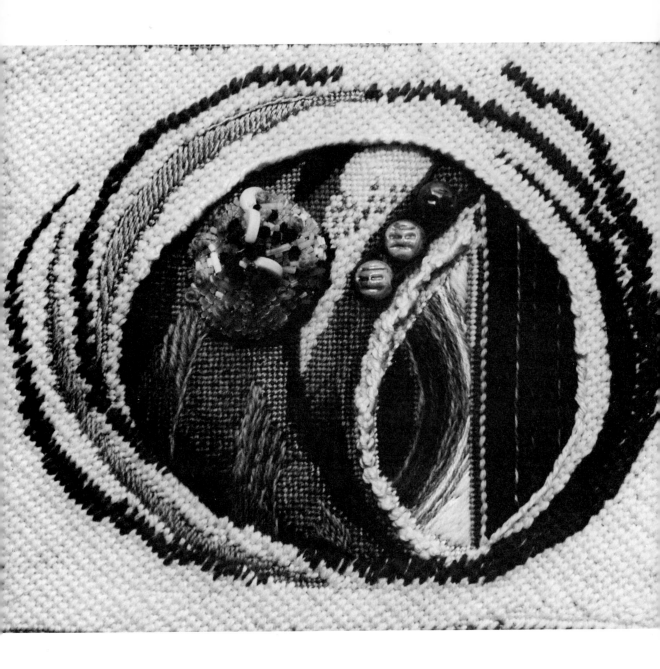

25 Design based on the curved shape of a cheese carton. To the left and slightly above the centre is a raised pyramid of canvas, covered closely with white glass beads and french knots and attached securely into position upon the background canvas. The outer background is in small diagonal stitch. The materials used were stranded cotton, silk, wool and perlita

26　Strips of thin card of various widths and lengths placed to suggest a design

27　Polythene bottle cut into rings and grouped

28　Thin card and polythene shapes together suggest an interesting design

29   Strips of corrugated paper, folded and grouped

30   Plaiting thin brown paper over and under suggests a textured stitch
for the background to a design to be worked in a flatter type of stitch

31

32

33

33a

34

30

31 Texture in cut paper

32 Square of paper folded diagonally and cut from the folded side into the middle

33 Folded square of paper cut to give an attractive open pattern

33a Folded square of paper cut to give a pattern, then divided into two parts and rearranged

34 Folded and cut paper shape

35 The same design as 34, cut and rearranged

36 A further rearrangement of design 34, resulting in another different design. Many more designs could be obtained from this one

37 An arrangement of the odd pieces remaining after the design above had been cut out of the original paper

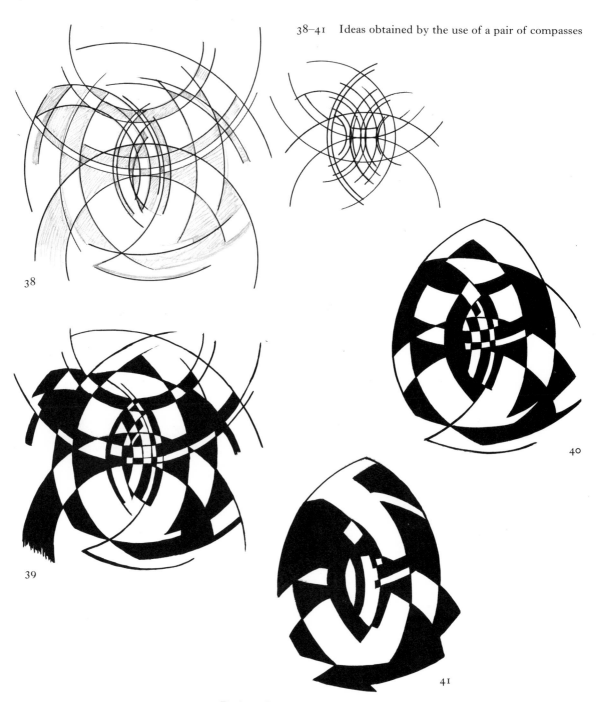

38

40

39

41

39 Design 38 traced with some lines thickened, others deleted

40 Design traced again and simplified. It could be simplified further

41 The design traced on to canvas could be worked in a variety of stitches

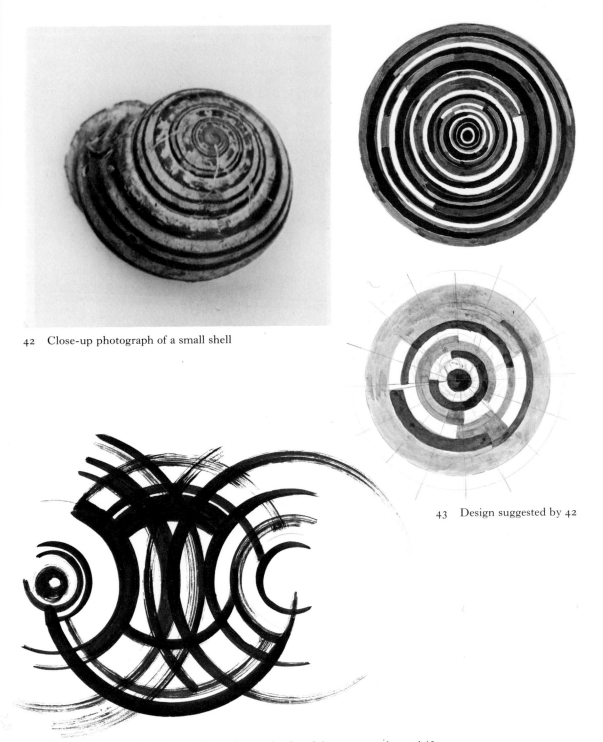

42 Close-up photograph of a small shell

43 Design suggested by 42

44 Construction of circles obtained by using a paint-brush in a compass instead of a pencil. By this means a great variety of thicknesses of line can be achieved

45

46

45   Interesting designs obtained from diagrams in scientific books

46   A newspaper advertisement cut and rearranged

47

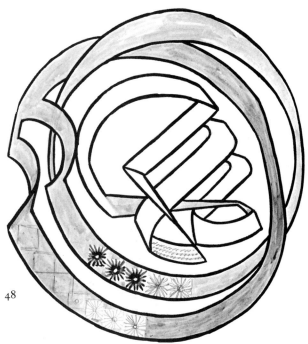

48

47   A doodle using a short length of charcoal or chalk crayon

48   Design based on previous sketch

Another possible method of obtaining a design, and one that is quite an old idea, is to cut or tear a small hole of from $\frac{1}{2}$ in. to 1 in. in diameter in a piece of paper—this is known as a finder—and to move this around on top of illustrations or advertisements in the glossy magazines or art books, and particularly in Sunday colour supplements, thus isolating small sections of the underlying pictures or advertisements until an interesting and satisfying design is discovered through the small aperture. These small sections can be very much enlarged by making a free drawing of them on to paper, when quite useful suggestions for an abstract design may well emerge, and often a ready-made colour scheme is provided by the original illustration.

49   Finder with sketches obtained from its use

50 Palm tree from a BOAC advertisement. Circle
indicates area chosen by 'finder'

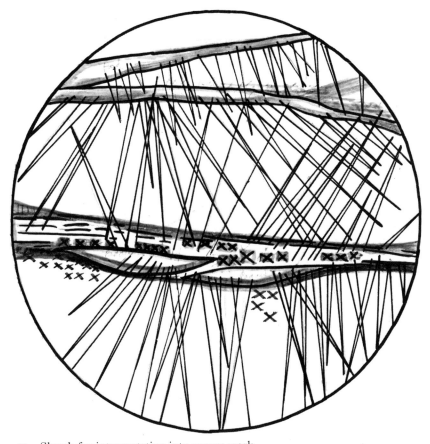

51 Sketch for interpretation into canvas work

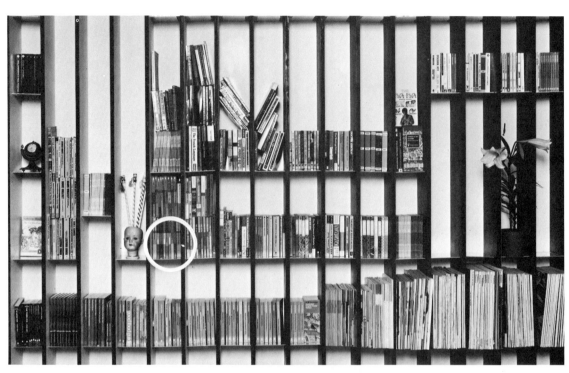

52

53

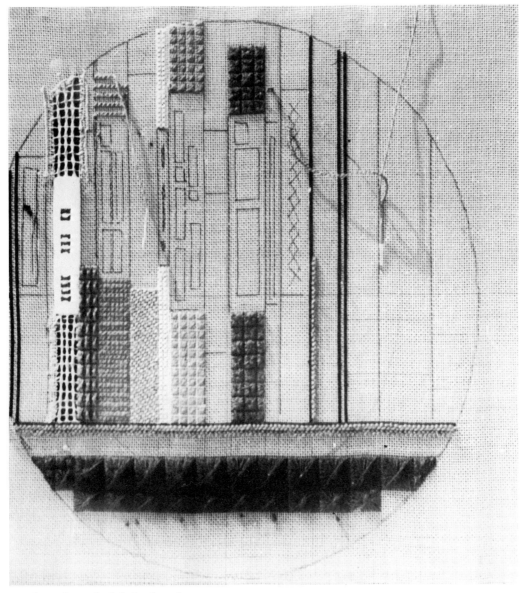

54 A partly worked design based on 53

Opposite
52 Circle indicates a section of paper-back books chosen with a finder from a magazine advertisement

53 Sketch for interpretation into canvas work. This design can be worked in a mixture of drawn threads and a wide variety of canvas stitches in wool, cotton and silk. The lines of the bookcase can be either drawn threads or applied threads, such as a quantity of canvas threads or creosoted string couched down in a decorative way

Ink blots on paper offer yet another and amusing way of finding a suggestion for a design which could be useful not only for canvas work, but for all types of embroidery. Fold a sheet of paper and, having opened it out again and placed it flat on the table in front of you, drop small blots of ink of varying sizes along the fold. Carefully fold the paper over again and press gently, using the finger-nail to ease the ink out in different directions. By doing this very carefully, you can to a certain extent guide

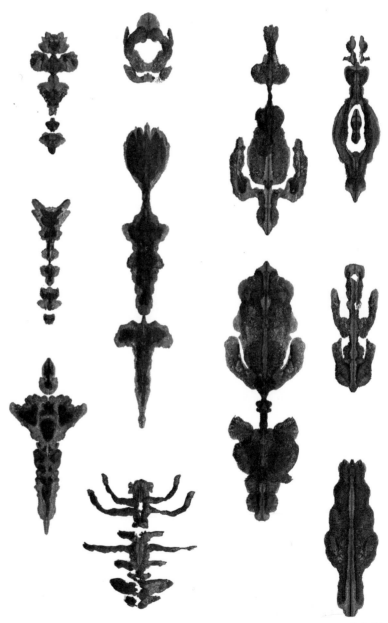

55 Ink blots

the line formed by the ink in any direction. When the ink has been pressed out to its fullest extent, open out the paper and, if necessary, add more ink blots, preferably of another colour, and repeat the process. When a satisfying result has been produced in this way, place a piece of thin paper over it and trace the design through. This design will then have to be greatly enlarged, if it is to be used for canvas work, and this can be done either by freehand drawing or by the squaring-up method of enlargement.

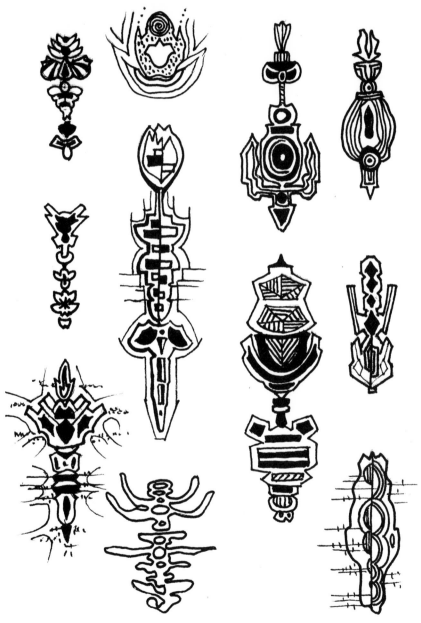

56   Designs developed from ink blots

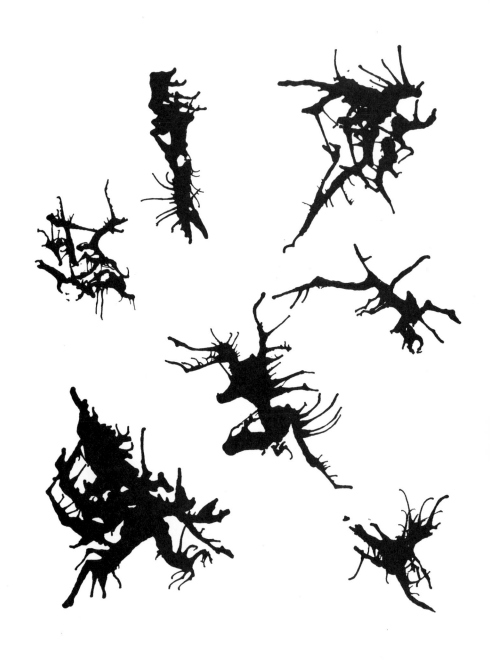

57　Blown ink blots

Doodling should not be despised as a source for embroidery designs. From a number of small doodles drawn on a sheet of paper the best can be selected and enlarged up to the size required for a design, additional lines then being drawn in to break up any areas in the enlarged drawing which seem lacking in interest. In doing this it is important to have in mind the decorative value of certain areas of undecorated space. Doodles formed by drawing a continuous line, or by arranging a length of string upon a plain background, can likewise lead to pleasing designs.

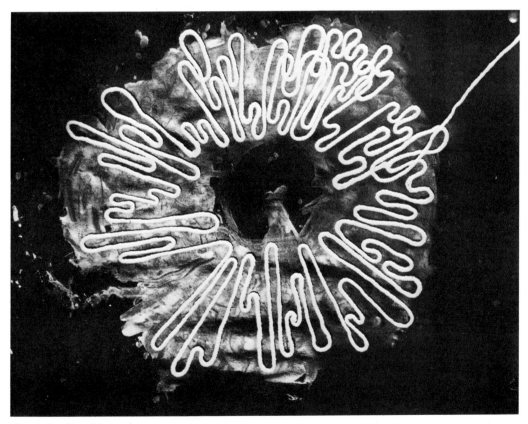

58   A doodle with wool

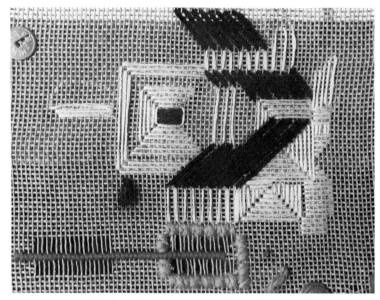

59 Black and white lines together with some drawn threads

60 Straight lines in black and white

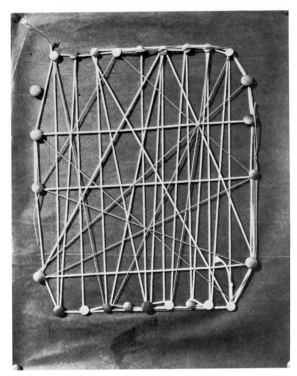

62

61   A doodle with string

62   Design based on 61 to be carried out in black and white and one strong
colour such as red or purple in a variety of stitches

63   Partly worked design in white and creosoted string, couched down

A further source of inspiration for a design can sometimes be found by cutting with a knife a cross-section of a fruit, a vegetable or the seed pod of a plant, and inspecting this cross-section under a powerful magnifying glass, or putting a very thin section of it on to a projection slide and photographing the silhouette formed when the slide is projected on to the screen. The patterns thus revealed are often very exciting and can lead to wonderful results in the production of designs for embroidery. Recently I used with good effect in a canvas-work panel a design suggested by the pith taken from the centre of a melon and laid out to dry on paper. See colour plate opposite page 49.

64

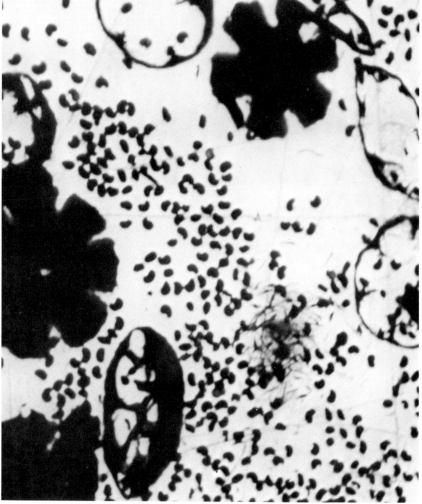

65 Section of a poppy head and its seeds, placed between glass, projected on to a screen and photographed

64 Shredded cabbage and other vegetables, can often suggest an idea for a workable design

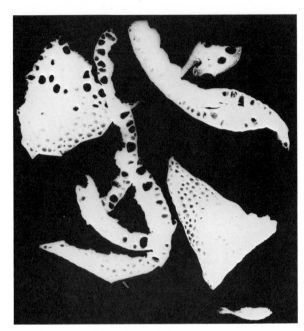

66 Orange peel forming a design

67 Sketch for canvas-work panel based on the above orange-peel design

68   Needlework panel, the design of which
was based on a grapefruit pip   *Lilian Hill*

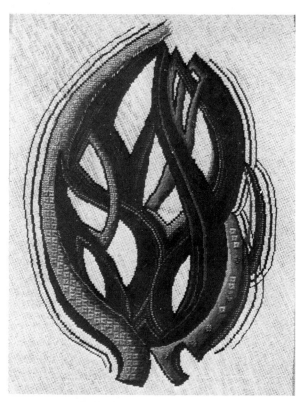

69   Travellers' joy enlarged by projection and photographed

Galaxy
This panel is an excellent and colourful example of the way in which stained glass and copper wire can be used to embellish a piece of canvas work. The background is rice stitch worked with rya wool and the rest of the design is carried out in Shetland wool and silk
Zena Halliwell

Blue Glass
Panel based on a design taken from melon pith
Mary Rhodes

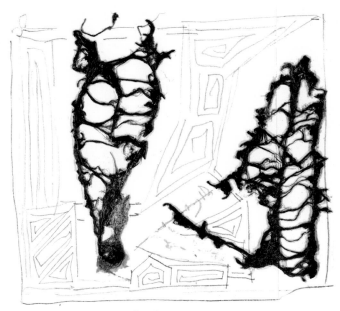

70 Dried membrane of melon

71 Sketch of dried melon pith. See colour plate opposite page 49

74 Sketches of birds, showing stylised treatment

Opposite
72 Sketches of shells showing ways of integrating shapes into the background.
No attempt should be made to treat these in a naturalistic manner

73 A freely adapted shell design with a multi-coloured background in pastel
shades, worked in long-legged cross stitch and giving the effect of mother of pearl
Lilian Hill

75 Symmetrical design. Designing with the aid of a mirror

Good results are also often obtained by observing the patterns formed by the sun shining through curtains or the branches of a tree on to a wall or the ground, or, of course, by observing the patterns of branches and twigs against the sky. A wineglass held up to the light can likewise suggest beautiful shapes which may be used for a design. The aspirant designer must always be on the watch for such sources of inspiration from Nature and the everyday world around us, where often apparently quite unpromising objects will suddenly reveal material which the imagination can successfully develop into most pleasing pieces of work. Shapes seen in industry, for instance, can often provide a fruitful source of ideas for both geometric and free designs on canvas: such things as pylons, scaffolding, cranes, timber yards, various types of machinery and even photographs from industrial magazines and newspapers can all yield exciting shapes which the alert designer can develop into successful designs for canvas embroidery.

Opposite
77 Sketch based on reflections of garden chairs. Take a portion of a reflection, such as this one, and repeat it. Then try reversing it, move it around, or turn it upside down or sideways until it links up. Eventually something workable will emerge which can be traced on to canvas and worked in suitable stitchery

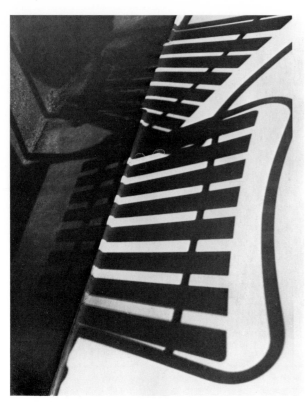

76 Reflections of garden chairs

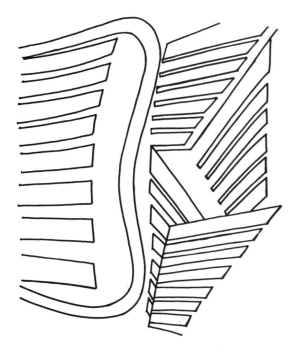

78   Reflections on a wall

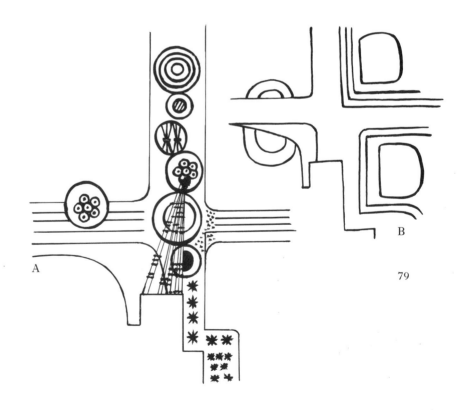

A

B

79

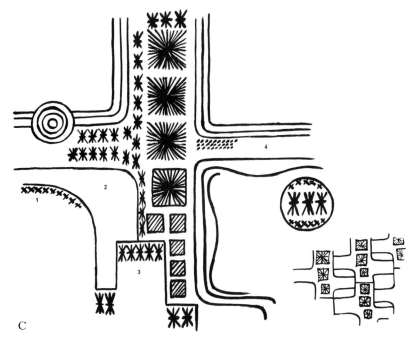

C

1 Cross stitch
2 Mosaic stitch
3 Wheatsheaf stitch
4 Tent stitch

79   Sketches based on reflections on a wall. *Sketch A* could be carried out with beads
and stitchery with strands of silk stretching from the beads. The strands of silk could
be woven in certain places *Sketch B* Some of these areas could be either padded or cut
away *Sketch C* suggestion for the starting-point of a design which can be developed
and extended to obtain a fair-sized design

80   Reflection of a lamp on a wall

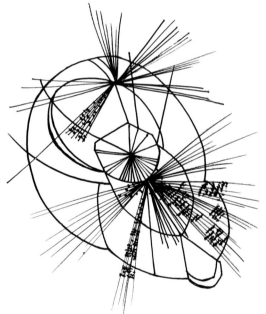

81   Sketch for design based on the reflection on a wall. Strands of silk or cotton stretched from a large bead on a raised padded section of a design and partly woven or darned can give added interest to a design. The drawing has purposely been made much rounder in form than the photograph (80). This is done because lines coming slightly off the straight of the canvas tend to look awkward, and a much better effect is obtained if the lines of the design are either kept strictly angular and worked on the straight of the canvas or alternatively definitely curved

56

82 A metal spring and its shadow suggest a design to be developed for canvas work

83 Reflection of rose hips

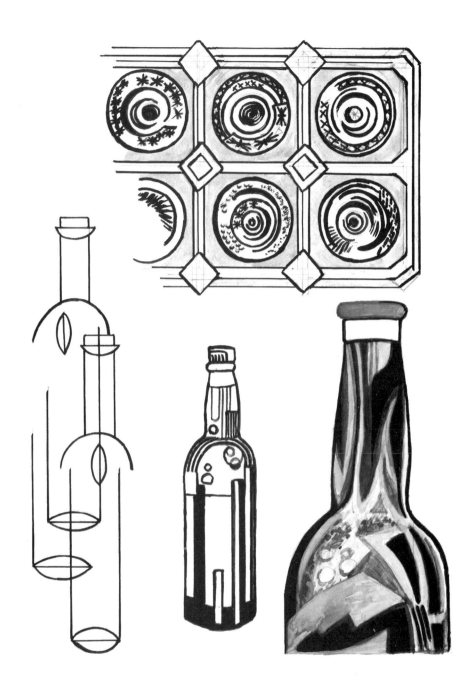

84 Sketches from reflections in a bottle and bottles in a bin

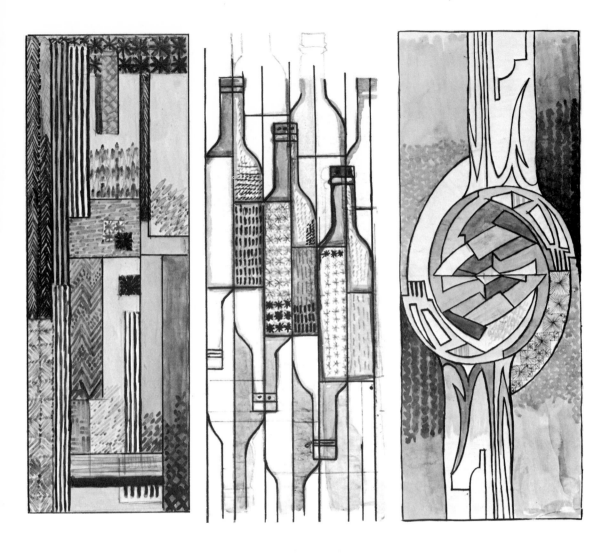

85   Three designs suitable for stool tops, based on these reflections

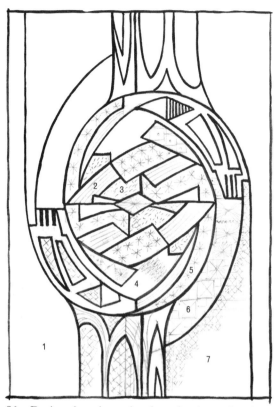

86 Design based on bottle reflections showing suggested stitches

    1   Long-legged stitch
    2   Alternate rows of tent stitch in two shades of colour
    3   Speckling
    4   Diagonal stitch
    5   Smyrna stitch
    6   Rhodes stitch
    7   Rice stitch

87 Design for a small panel based on the bottle and its reflection

    1   Florentine stitch
    2   Diagonal stitch
    3   Cross stitch
    4   Milanese stitch
    5   Rhodes stitch
    6   Cushion stitch
    7   Tent stitch
    8   Eye stitch
    9   Basket stitch

88 Blown-up photograph of a box of sequins. Another possible source of a design

89

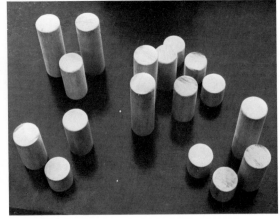

91

90

92

89   The dark areas formed by these small blocks of wood, together with the medium and light tones, could make a most interesting design. The grain of the wood also suggests stitches that might be used, such as rice, Parisian and diagonal stitches

90   Small lengths of dowel rod grouped and photographed

91   This photograph of short lengths of rod suggests an exciting three-dimensional design

92   A group of match-boxes

93

94

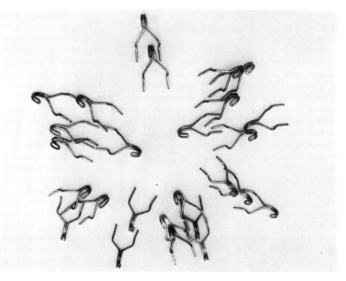

95

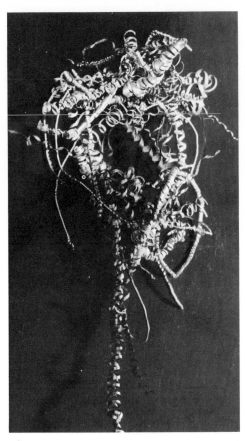

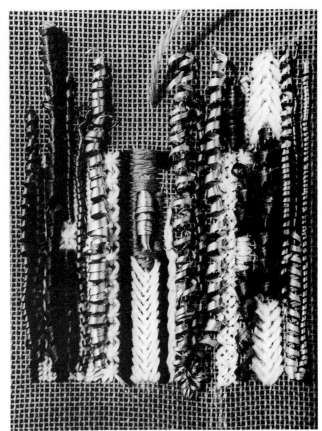

96   97

96   Waste metal filings suggest the free use of textural stitches

97   Pieces of waste metal used in conjunction with stitchery

Opposite
93   Scrap of metal binding from a case of wine

94   A bead necklace. Unusual beads can often give inspiration

95   Peg-board pins, such as these, paper clips, match-sticks, dropped at random
on a board, can suggest a design

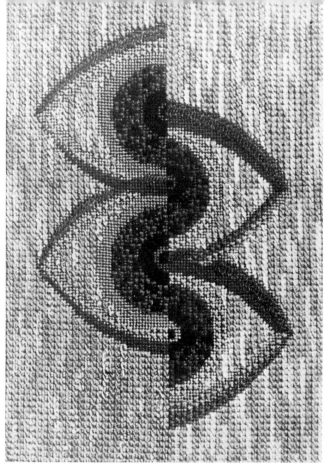

98 Design based on the human eye and worked on canvas. The background is worked in long-legged cross stitch in shades of pink and orange silk and wool
Lilian Hill

99 This is another design based on the human eye. The design is quartered and worked in rice and Parisian stitches with wool, silk and nylon raffia. A design suitable for a cushion   *Lilian Hill*

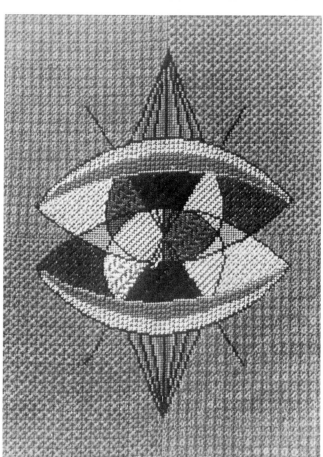

100   Designing directly on to canvas. This design was developed by placing paper, copper waste, tin-can tops and fish-paste fasteners directly on to the canvas and adding lines, both thick and thin, in black paint. A free design of this type when worked can either incorporate the actual metal pieces or these can be discarded and be replaced by stitchery. Some of the smaller circles could be padded or covered with material such as lurex, or gold, silver or other leather. The background could be worked or left unworked

101   Design built up directly on to canvas. This comprises strips of copper, aluminium and paper. The background and pattern are of equal importance in this type of design and as much care and attention should be taken with the spacing of the background as with the pattern

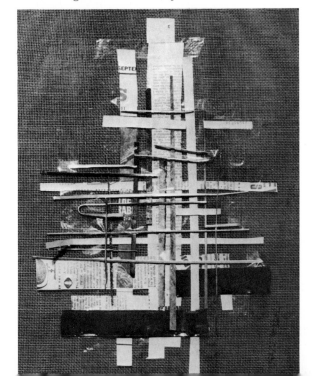

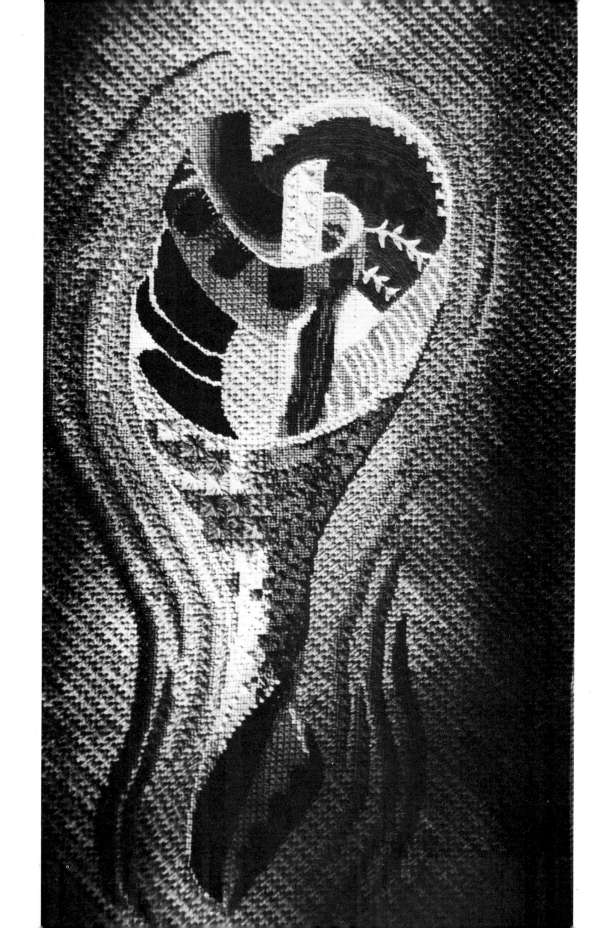

A visit to a museum can be a rich source of inspiration to the embroidery designer. Not only can benefit be derived from the study of the tapestries and embroideries to be found for example in the Victoria and Albert Museum, London, but such objects as mosaics, illuminated manuscripts, stained glass, book-bindings, pottery, enamels and ivories can also provide a wonderful stimulus and a fund of ideas for the designer.

It generally takes a little time for the beginner to achieve a good, balanced design. I believe that the main thing to remember in the initial stages of designing is to keep everything in the design as simple as possible and to avoid having the area of background exactly the same size as the area of pattern. Then, when it is felt that the basis for a good, well-balanced design has been obtained, with shapes that are attractive, varied and well placed in the space to be covered, extra lines may be inserted to add further detail and fill out and complete the final drawing.

Embroidery designs today tend to avoid the symmetrical as being too traditional, and, therefore, the asymmetrical is now what is most popular —that is, designs with their main elements placed slightly off centre. This certainly gives greater freedom of line and leads to a preponderance of abstract designs; it can, however, bring about a great weakness in design if certain areas are allowed to become unbalanced. In order to combat a tendency to unbalance it is as a general rule good practice to ensure that lines in a design which slope in one direction are balanced by other lines sloping in the opposite direction.

In cases where so-called 'found' objects are used in present-day canvas embroidery, these objects can either form the basis for the original design without themselves being actually employed as an integral part of the finished work—this is shown in the panel (73), where a shell, found on the beach, was the inspiration for the design—or they can themselves be directly incorporated into the finished piece of work, as in the examples shown in *Skanes* (103) and *Sea Shells* (212).

When it is found necessary to include human figures in a canvas-work panel, these should be treated very simply and in a more or less decorative manner. They should on no account be treated naturalistically. In the first place a naturalistic treatment is quite undesirable in this medium, and in any case it is not possible to render satisfactorily such details as those of flesh and hair in this way within the very limited scope of the materials used.

Opposite : Skeleton Shell
102   Curved lines are sometimes difficult for the beginner to work, but providing the curve is first outlined with tent stitch no difficulty should arise   *Rose Cussens*

Opposite

103   *Skanés* (unfinished). This piece of work evolved on the canvas with no design.
It started with the circle at the bottom and was built up gradually from there. Lovely
stones with holes in them, found on a holiday beach and just waiting to be sewn on to
the canvas were the inspiration. String, wooden beads and wool were added. The
background will probably be left unworked

104   *Madder* panel detail. Figure treated stylistically with a very simple treatment
used for working the face with no attempt at naturalism   *Lilian Hill*

105 *Bus Queue*. A group of children worked in a variety of stitches   *Lilian Hill*

Opposite
106 *Seated figure*. Stylised figure. When working a figure it is sometimes more interesting to elongate it or parts can be enlarged or reduced   *Lilian Hill*

70

107 *Dancing Women*. Depicting almost complete denial of naturalism
Winnie Browning

108 *Woman with flowers*. Very simple lines filled mainly with diagonal stitch on background of mosaic stitch *Lilian Hill*

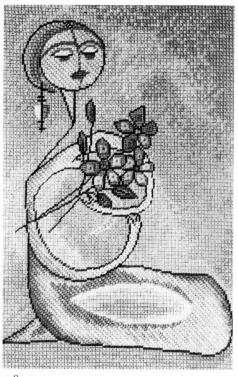

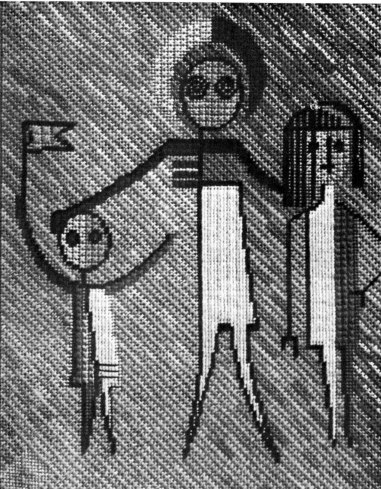

109 *Three figures*. Designed and worked very simply in a variety of stitches *Lilian Hill*

108

London
A panel 3 ft 3 in. × 2 ft 6 in., showing the use of a variety of stitches in a decorative
representation of famous buildings in and around London   *Miriam Bawden*

Free stitchery
Tufts of wool are tied down on a background of straight stitches

110 *Face of a girl*. Worked mainly in mosaic stitch   *Miriam Bawden*

111   *Madonna* panel. Traditional figures. This design was taken from a Christmas
card, enlarged and adapted to canvas work   *Rose Cussens*

Opposite
112   Detail from *Madonna* panel. The figure is picked out in white silk on a variegated
background of tent stitch

113 *Mosaic* panel. A very long and narrow panel in which many small varied designs are arranged around a cross, superimposed upon a sun. The colouring is mainly in blues, greens and mauves, worked in silk and wool in a variety of stitches (size 24 in. × 73 in.)

Lilian Hill

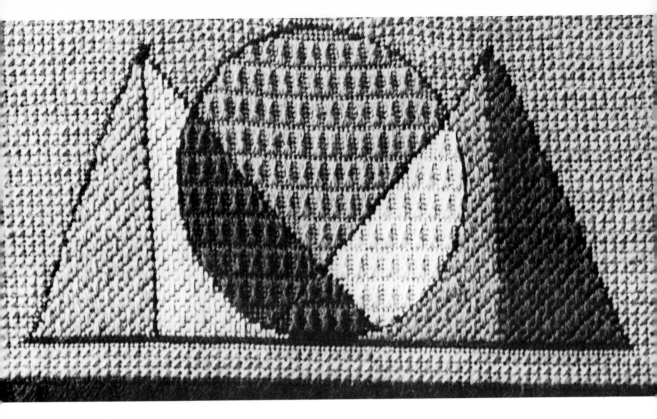

114–16 Details of the 'mosaic' panel

117   Detail from *London* panel. See colour plate opposite page 72

3 The transition from conventional to modern methods of designing and working

Until after the close of the Second World War canvas embroidery remained very traditional in nature: people with the leisure to do so worked innumerable chair seats, stool tops, valances, bell pulls, etc, all designed in the conventional manner. The stitches used continued to be almost exclusively tent stitch and cross stitch, and the designs largely floral.

118   Reproduction eighteenth-century chair seat, one of a set of six. This shows a sense of symmetrical balance combined with technical skill which has produced a design which is very suitable for its purpose   *Dorothy Hassock*

During the past twenty years, however, there has been a great change which has carried canvas embroidery away from the very low ebb it had reached between the two world wars. This change was part of the greatly altered attitude of all artists and craftsmen, who now began to move away from traditional modes of expression into wide new fields of creativity. An international exchange of styles in art took place and ideas penetrated into England, particularly from the United States of America, which has played a major role in the evolution to a new contemporary style.

As a result of this world-wide development and interchange of ideas in art, canvas work, together with all other forms of embroidery, moved away from its traditional confines to adopt a much more experimental attitude, which was further assisted as time went on by the use of a much greater diversity of materials.

Perhaps the first indications of the change to a more modern attitude in canvas work is to be seen in the use of pictorial rather more than floral motifs, and the accompanying tendency to depict modern scenes of everyday life rather than the more stylised 'period' pieces of earlier days, which had been felt appropriate when the work was executed especially for coverings on antique or reproduction furniture. Not only were pictorial scenes of modern life now accepted, but the actual treatment of natural forms in such scenes became more bold and vigorous; colour probably played a very large part in this transformation, as one now tended not to adhere so closely to the traditional range of five shades for each colour, and this caused a much greater contrast of light and shade than had formerly been the case. The treatment of backgrounds in modern pictorial pieces, especially with regard to the use of colour, was also very different: brighter colours were employed and a textured treatment of the background areas by means of rapid changes of colour was gradually introduced. (See figure 119.)

As in other art forms, so in canvas embroidery, the final break with tradition in design came with the acceptance of the purely abstract. The canvas itself began to be used in a much freer way: it did not any longer require to be completely covered with worked stitches; it could be cut into a variety of shapes; jewels, gold leather, velvet and other materials, as well as 'found' objects, could be attached to it; areas of worked canvas could be raised above the background; threads of the canvas could be withdrawn; coloured glass and other types of background material could be allowed to show through openings in the canvas; in fact, many devices which were coming into use in other forms of embroidery were now found to be equally applicable to canvas work. Today very much work of an experimental nature is being carried out, and it is not clear in what direction future trends will move.

Opposite

119   *Seashore.* A detail of a large panel, showing present-day treatment which is bolder, freer and dispenses with the fine delicate shading of the old designs

Lilian Hill

120   This small panel shows sections of the canvas cut away to reveal pink antique glass. The cut edges are oversewn so that no bare canvas is visible. Other areas are padded and are covered with gold kid. The rest of the panel is worked mainly in satin, large and small Smyrna and tent stitches, in shades of grey, pink, magenta, yellow and black

Marjorie Chalk

121   Detail of canvas partly worked, showing areas to be cut away to reveal a background of coloured glass. It is intended to superimpose very small blocks of glass, not only on the background glass itself, but also on the lower part of the design. The canvas under these will remain uncut

Molly Revetto

119

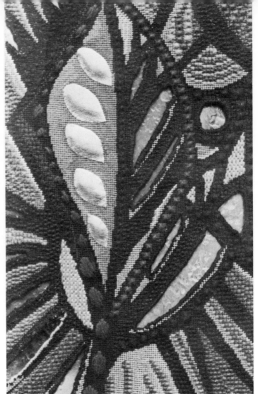

120

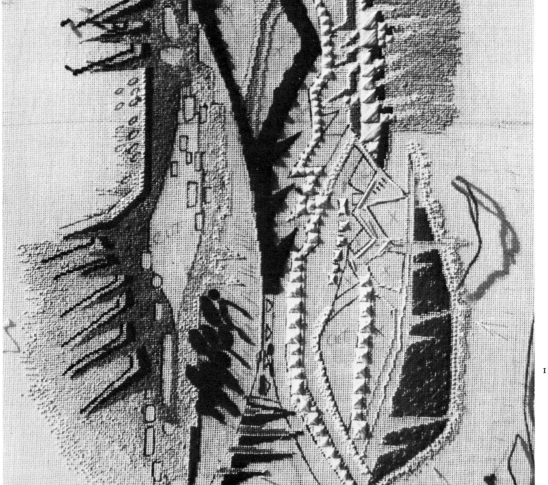

121

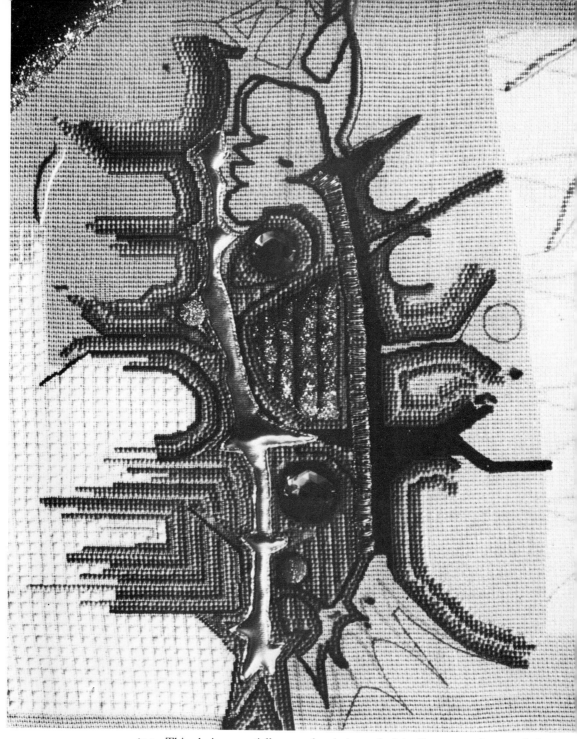

122 This design, partially completed, is worked in Smyrna and tent stitches
together with areas of padded gold lurex material and gold orion cloth, which is
overlapped with gold thread. Two large topaz jewels are incorporated

Opposite
123 Design 122 when completely worked *Florence Hawes*

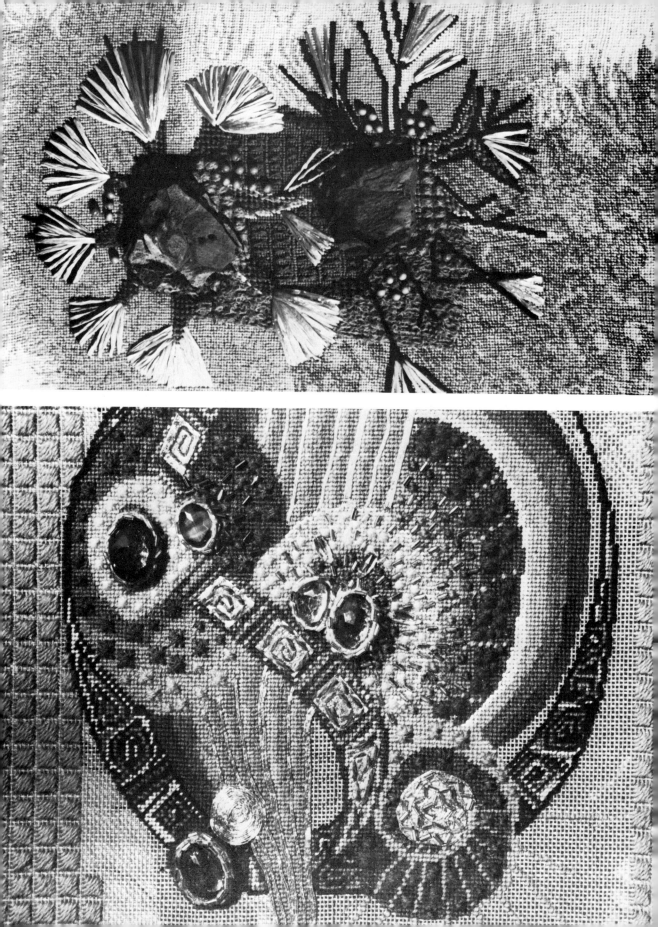

126 Ormer shells, or sea ears, are here shown sewn on to canvas through the natural holes in the shells, the outsides of which are padded in order to bring them back to the level of the canvas, so they can be more fully integrated into the background
Mary Fairbanks

Opposite
124 Small pieces of tree bark and wooden beads were incorporated in this design, together with raffia and bouclé wool. This small panel has an interesting background worked in tent stitch, which is very skilfully blended in many shades of blue
Daisy Chamberlin

125 Gold kid, gold thread, jewels, beads, silk and wool were used to work this panel. The colouring is in shades of yellow and green, whilst the background, which is in cushion stitch, is in a light shade of madder red   *Mildred Maguire*

127

128

129

130

Opposite

127 A baby owl, the design of which was taken from a colour photograph. It is worked in a somewhat naturalistic manner in tent stitch whilst the surrounding greenery is treated more stylistically by the use of a variety of stitches

Sheila Gibson

128 This is worked quite simply in cross and tent stitch in shades of madder brown and the whole design is heavily out-lined with blue filoselle silk. The Hungarian stitch background is worked in shades of blue, while the leaves, in eyelet stitch, are in two shades of sage green *Winifred Jury*

129 Although this owl appears to be somewhat naturalistic in appearance, apart from the colouring, there was no conscious attempt at naturalism and the finished piece of work could not be mistaken for anything other than a piece of needlework

Dorothy Hassock

130 *Blue Owl.* Satin and tent stitches are used for this bird, while the background includes large diagonal, Rhodes and tent stitches. The colouring is almost entirely carried out in blues, blue-green and black. *Lilian Hill*

It is interesting to compare the different ways of working these four owls

131 *Fish.* Worked in string and wool. The string has been dyed with natural dyestuffs and the background is left unworked. It is mounted in a box frame covered with canvas with strands of Bernat Klein wool criss-crossing the surface. The edges of the box frame are covered with plaits of creosoted string *Lilian Hill*

4 Colour, textures and stitches

Colour

From the earliest times colour has been important in the lives of human beings and it remains a source of delight to nearly everyone. It can be very exciting, joyful or even dramatic; it can be harmonious and soothing; it can induce a feeling of calmness; it can reflect sadness and despair. Thus, when used in a work of art, colour can help the artist or designer to create atmosphere, to suggest a pleasant sensation or the reverse, warmth or coldness, darkness or light. He can use it so that the effect is completely static, or he can make the lines of colour mingle and flow in a swirling representation of natural movement. The way in which he does this, however, must always remain a very individual matter, as, despite the numerous theories of colour harmony which have been propounded, and which do give helpful suggestions, there are no absolutely hard-and-fast rules which can be generally applied to the use of colour. The individual must in the end decide for himself what effect he wishes to achieve, must look at Nature and apply the information he gathers from its wealth of colour in the way he feels best suited to the medium he is using, whether it be paint or wool or silk, and create his own world of colour. Only thus has he a chance to bring originality and freshness to his work.

Simple natural objects provide some of the most important sources of colour schemes for artistic works. If flowers and birds, butterflies and moths, shells and stones, water and sunsets and the many other elements of Nature are carefully examined and detailed notes of their colouring are taken, these will provide the stimulus for designs at some later date. In studying such natural objects for this purpose, it should always be remembered that not only the more brilliantly coloured ones will yield useful results, but that those which have a more subdued colouring, when looked at very closely, will often reveal colour schemes just as interesting.

When we consider the atmosphere suggested by colours, it is clear that the so-called warm colours, red, orange and yellow, which are related in Nature to sunlight, fire and warmth, are also the colours which in an artistic creation suggest vigour and excitement, whilst the blues and greens, the so-called cool colours, which are associated with the sky, the sea and natural vegetation, with shadows and the absence of sunlight, are those which suggest calm and rest.

When actual colour schemes are being worked out, it is of course necessary to bear in mind certain simple principles of colour mixing and colour juxtaposition. Red, yellow and blue are the three primary colours from which all the other colours are made. By mixing red and yellow orange is obtained, from red and blue comes purple, whilst yellow and blue together give green. Purple, orange and green are known as the complementary colours: purple is the complementary colour to yellow, orange to blue and green to red. When two of the complementary colours are mixed together, the tertiary colours are obtained, orange and green giving citron, purple and green giving olive and orange and purple giving russet. Finally, when a primary colour is mixed with its complementary colour, a corresponding shade of grey is obtained. It is, also, very important to remember that the character of a colour can be changed completely by the nature of its surroundings, and it is, therefore, only possible to retain the characteristic effect of a particular single colour by outlining it with areas of black or white, which are neutral in effect and isolate the colour in question. It should not be overlooked, however, that most colours will appear rather brighter, and the area they cover will appear smaller, when placed on a black background than when placed on a white one. From this it follows, when canvas work is being done, that, in order to intensify the darkness of a colour, it should be contrasted with a light-coloured silk highlight, and that, in order to produce the effect of greater brightness, it should be placed against a very dark shade.

If we consider further the effect of placing various colours next to one another, we find other similar cases of one colour influencing the nature of another. As we might expect, a pale yellow will cause a red to appear richer, and a purple will cause it to seem paler. This effect is not, however, merely the result of contrast, but is induced by what is known as the after-image, which is the colour temporarily seen after the eye has been stimulated for a while by another colour. This after-image can be seen most clearly, if one looks immediately from a coloured object to a white or neutral-coloured surface, when the after-image appears in the colour which is complementary to the one originally observed. This effect is often made use of, for example, in the well-known practice of serving a green salad on a cool pink or red plate, when the greenness of the salad appears to be intensified, or of using a specific green tablecloth to make the meats served at dinner appear a richer brown and generally to enhance the appearance of the food. In canvas work, too, it can be observed, that, even when a neutral grey is used next to green it will appear pinkish, whilst against a red it will acquire a greenish hue.

It is generally necessary, when starting a new piece of canvas work, to try out several colour schemes before deciding on what is finally the most suitable. The time thus spent, however long it may seem, is not wasted, as it is very helpful in training the eye to see what are satisfactory colour harmonies. Thin coloured papers, or better still a variety of coloured fabrics, are most useful for trying out colour schemes, as well as for discovering interesting designs. It is best to start by taking quite tiny snippets of the chosen materials and assembling them in certain ranges of colour. From these ranges a colour scheme can be obtained by selecting materials, either in one colour range, or in one colour range with a hint of the complementary colour, or even in contrasting colours, and by dropping them at random on a chosen background, if there is as yet no preconceived design, or by arranging them on a suitable background, if a design is already in mind. In order to keep the colour scheme lively, it is necessary to watch that sufficient variety of tone, which is the degree of density or luminosity of a colour, is introduced into the scheme, as otherwise a flatness of effect will occur. On the other hand, the designer must beware of an unbalanced use of contrasting tones, which can easily destroy the unity of a design. When developing a colour scheme using contrasting colours, it is better to limit the number of colours used, as too many different colours tend to produce a confusing effect. In arranging contrasting colours next to one another it is often helpful to try placing a light-medium shade of one colour against a dark shade of the contrasting colour or a dark shade of the one against a very pale shade of the other, and if ranges of colours are being used, it is a good idea to try placing the first three light shades of one colour against the two darkest shades of an entirely different colour. By experimenting in this way one discovers that colours as far apart as yellow and purple can together yield an attractive range of colour provided that the gradation of tone is clearly defined.

Interesting effects involving combinations of colour can be achieved when canvas embroidery is actually being worked by mixing thin threads of different shades of wool or silk. This idea can be especially useful for backgrounds in canvas work. For instance, if a reddish-purple wool and a deep gold-coloured wool are used together in the needle, the finished effect, when viewed from a distance, will be that of a rich burnt sienna; strands of red and green or of orange and blue will give grey, but they will appear much livelier than would a single flat grey wool.

Colours which are to be used in working chair seats and furnishings should always be kept on the bright side to allow for fading, and in this connection it should be borne in mind that, despite any claims of permanence the manufacturers may make for their dyes, these will inevitably lose some of their brightness over a period of time. It cannot furthermore be too strongly stressed that one should beware of using for this purpose the so-called 'tapestry' shades of wool. These ranges of 'subtle' colours, arrived at originally by matching up from the already faded shades of early pieces of work, have been associated for many decades with canvas work and are still offered by many shops which deal in materials for this type of work. Their use can only lead to the very lifeless effect too often regarded as typical of canvas embroidery.

The natural or vegetable-dyed wools are to my mind the first choice for use in canvas work owing to the liveliness and vigour of their colours. Most scientists will deny that synthetic dyes are in any way inferior to natural dyes and will stress their greater permanence, but, having worked for many years with both naturally and synthetically dyed wools, I have come to the conclusion that the naturally dyed wools possess characteristics which make them superior for canvas work. The natural dyes do fade more quickly than synthetic dyes and the latter are, therefore, much better for use in expendable articles such as clothes, which have a limited life, but over the much longer periods of time during which pieces of canvas work can be expected to last the difference in the nature of the fading between synthetic and natural dyes becomes more apparent, and it is my experience that the natural dyes simply fade to a lighter shade of the same colour, whereas synthetic dyes, when they begin to fade, tend to do so in a completely unpredictable way: they often fade to a lifeless grey and in many cases the darker shades, particularly of blue, will fade to a grey which is lighter in tone than other medium shades used in the same piece of work. This drastic fading does not normally appear until after about five years, but, when it does happen, the tonal values in a colour-scheme can be completely destroyed, whereas, if natural dyes are employed, however much they fade, the colours retain the original tonal balance.

The difference between naturally dyed and synthetically dyed wools is particularly noticeable when they are used for working large areas of one colour, which happens for instance sometimes in working backgrounds. The synthetic dyes give a completely flat, unbroken effect, but the natural dyes are lively and vibrant as a result, I believe, of the very slight unevenness in the penetration of the dye. This effect of unevenness of colour is very often quite imperceptible in the skein, but, when the wool has been worked into a design, the colour is just sufficiently broken to yield the greater liveliness which is needed in a large area of one colour. In order to obtain a similar effect with synthetically dyed wools, it is necessary to use two shades of a colour which are very close to one another, and either to work with a strand of each shade together in the needle or to work alternate lines in a different shade.

Textures and stitches

Just as it is important to bear in mind tonal relationships when planning colour-schemes, and to realise that patterns made by variations of tone play a very vital part in a design, so it is also important to have a clear conception of the effect of textural variations in canvas work. Particular qualities of the materials being used, as well as the effects of certain canvas-work stitches, can be turned to advantage in a design, and it is essential to make sure that, when it is completed, an embroidered panel shall appear unmistakably to be an embroidery: the very worst thing that could be said about it would be: 'It is just like a painting!' It is far better to limit the number of colours in a design and to get the maximum effect from them by using a variety of stitches to give changes of tone and of texture. By using both large and small stitches in working an area of one colour it is possible to produce shadows, which in their turn can introduce considerable tonal variation. It is, however, necessary to hang a wall-panel or picture, in which this method of working has been employed, in a good light, preferably a side light, and it will then immediately come to life. If, on the other hand, such a panel is hung where little strong light reaches it, the work will appear flat and dull.

This use of textural effects in canvas work is, of course, one of its important features, but it should not be allowed to become indiscriminate, or, as I have already stated, ludicrous effects may be produced, especially when natural shapes are the main objects in a design, and the textures employed are not in keeping with these shapes or cause unpleasant distortion of them when viewed from a distance. The embroiderer must choose carefully the type of stitch which is best suited to each element in a design and not develop a preference for one type of stitch to the exclusion of others. This latter practice has resulted in the recent past in the predominance of square stitches to the exclusion of tent stitch, a development which probably owes a great deal to the production about 70 years ago of a book by Lewis F. Day and Mary Buckle called *Art in Needlework*. In this book the authors stated, among other things, that 'embroidery is merely an affair of stitching', and they concentrated on cross stitch and its variants as the main stitches to be used for canvas work, dismissing the wonderful canvas embroidery of the seventeenth century, worked in tent stitch, as 'painful object lessons in what not to do'.

I believe that this book, which has been widely read, and from which quotations are still made in many modern books on embroidery, has done more to destroy the true image of earlier canvas work and to affect adversely the technique of many modern canvas embroiderers than any other book in the history of the craft. If the authors' insistence on the use of square stitches is really based, as they maintain, on the belief that embroidery stitches should always bear a relationship to the material on which they are worked, then they should surely agree that tent stitch is just as suitable for the purpose of the canvas embroiderer as cross stitch, for it is, in fact, half a cross stitch and follows the diagonal of the canvas just as naturally as the various forms of cross stitch follow the warp and weft. It also has the advantage that it is much more adaptable for working curved lines and can be used to avoid the awkward 'stepped' effect so often seen in pieces of canvas work, an effect which Lewis Day seems to have felt was a desirable element in this kind of embroidery. The skilful use of tent stitch does, in fact, free the designer from the rather inhibiting effect of the square stitch, but he must always bear in mind that, if used to work large, unbroken areas of one colour, it will produce an insipid effect; he must, therefore, show his skill in combining its use with that of the great variety of other canvas stitches and with effective variations in colour and tone.

One thing to remember when working a plain tent-stitch background is that it is essential to work the rows of stitches either all horizontally or all vertically. If you start working the rows of stitches horizontally and then, after a while, decide to have a change and start working the rows vertically, the result will invariably be that the area, where the change of direction in the rows of stitches occurs, will appear on the front of the work as a patch. (See figure 148.)

132–8   A few natural objects from which ideas may be obtained for canvas work

132   Seed heads

133   Thistle

134   Flowering grass

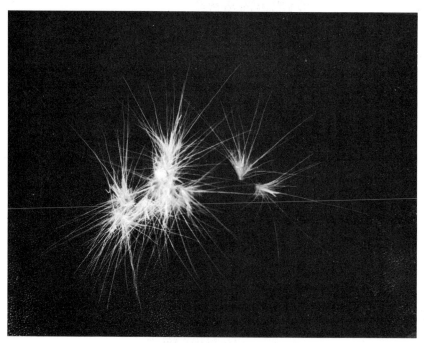

135 Details of flowering grass

136 Seed head of winter aconite much enlarged

137 and 138 Shells

139 Silver birch bark. Pieces of bark often show very interesting texture, and from them ideas may be obtained for textural effects with stitches

140 Cork. This shows a good suggestion for texture

141 Cherry bark. Rubbings with thin paper and heel ball of different types of tree bark can give ideas for background texture

Opposite
142 Miniature collages. These are enlargement photographs of small collages, measuring $1-1\frac{1}{2}$ in. square. Snippets of chosen materials, either dropped at random or arranged, and stuck down on thin card, are useful to suggest a scheme not only for colour, but also for texture and tonal values. A number of these models can be made and retained as a source of ideas for future reference

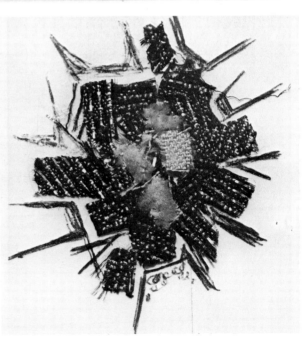

97

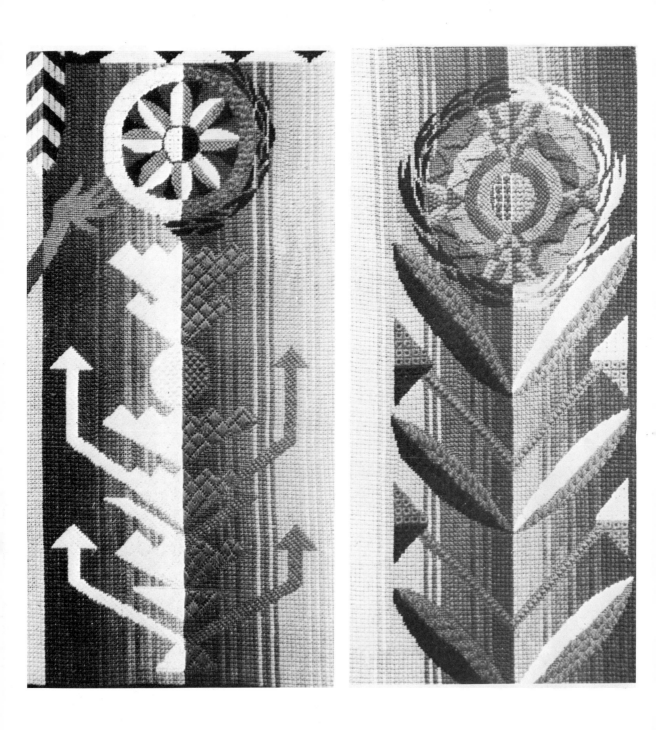

143 Detail of large panel showing strong tonal contrast and an interesting use of stitches

144 Another detail of the same panel

145 Tent stitch used to give a textured effect to a background by skilful merging of colours

146 A variation of tent stitch with stitches of different lengths, which achieves a remarkable textural effect

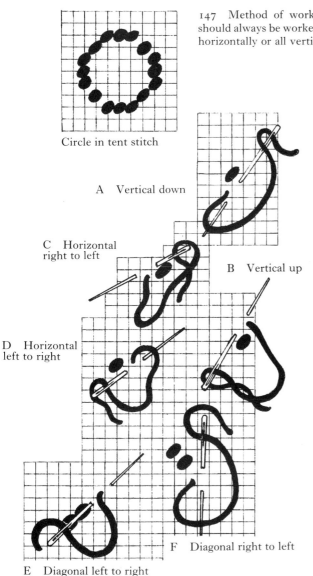

147 Method of working tent stitch. A large flat area of unbroken tent stitch should always be worked one way, i.e. either all the lines of stitches should be worked horizontally or all vertically

Circle in tent stitch

A   Vertical down

C   Horizontal
right to left

B   Vertical up

D   Horizontal
left to right

E   Diagonal left to right

F   Diagonal right to left

Free use of tent stitch
Interesting results can be obtained
by varying the length of the stitch

148 Wrong technique in working tent stitch. This photograph shows clearly the effect of working a block of 12 stitches horizontally and then suddenly changing to working the next block of stitches vertically. Although all the individual stitches slope in the same direction, the change of direction in working the lines of stitches results in a patch-like effect which will always be obvious in the finished work

149 Rococo stitch worked on 16-mesh congress canvas

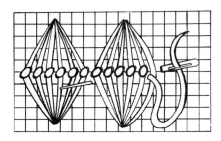

Rococo over 9 threads tied
down with tent stitch

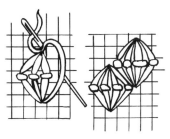

Stitch worked over 4 threads
tied down with back stitch on
coarse canvas

150 Method of working rococo stitch

151 Rococo stitch worked on flax
canvas

152   Rhodes stitch. This is a bold, chunky, square stitch which, when worked over 28 or more threads, is tied down across the corners, forming a diamond shape to give greater interest and variety

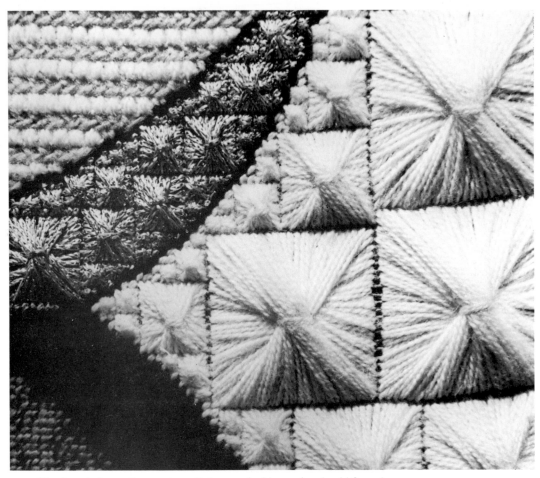

153   Rhodes stitch, medium and small size, worked in wool and gold fingering yarn

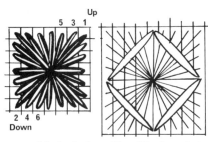

Extra large

154   Method of working Rhodes stitch

157 Hungarian stitch. Areas of Hungarian stitch, showing the hard edges of this stitch softened by the use of tent stitch

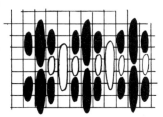

158 Method of working Hungarian stitch

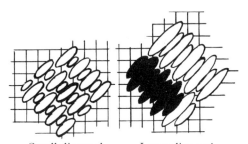

Small diagonal   Large diagonal

160 Method of working diagonal stitch

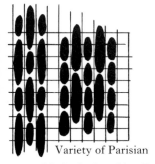

Variety of Parisian

159 Method of working Parisian stitch

Opposite
155 Hungarian stitch showing very skilful shading.
The circular shape is surrounded by wheatsheaf stitch.

156 Hungarian stitch on flax canvas

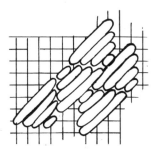

161 Method of working Milanese stitch

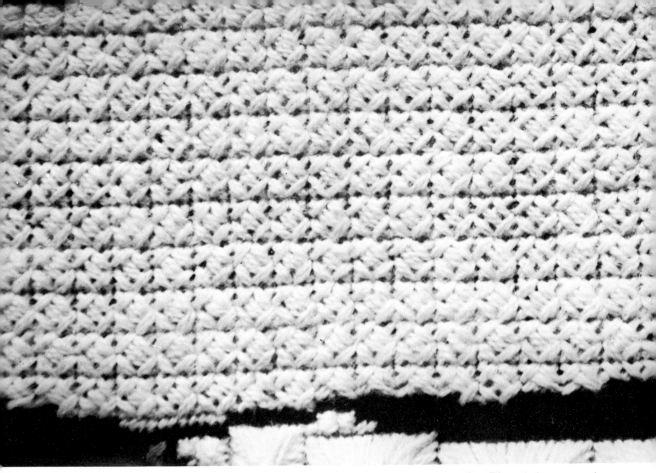

162 Rice stitch or crossed corners

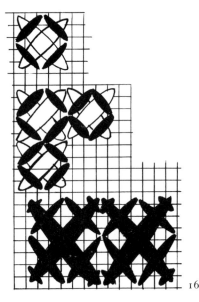

163 Method of working rice stitch

164   Vertical and horizontal diamond stitch

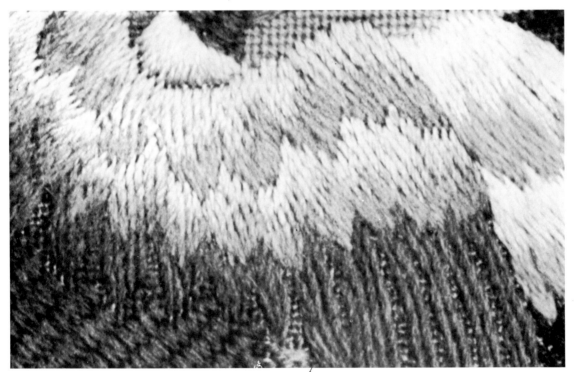

165   Stem stitch. Detail of bird's wing worked in stem stitch with a background in diagonal stitch

166   Large diamond and bullion stitches

167   Portuguese stem stitch. A motif in Portuguese stem stitch and tent stitch with a background in Italian three-sided and fan stitches

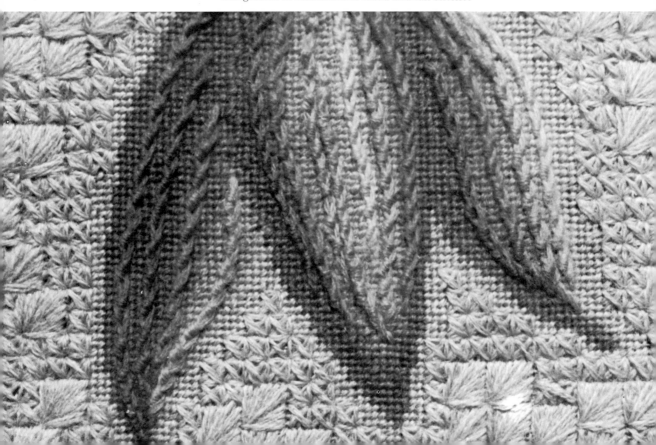

The black stitch is worked last

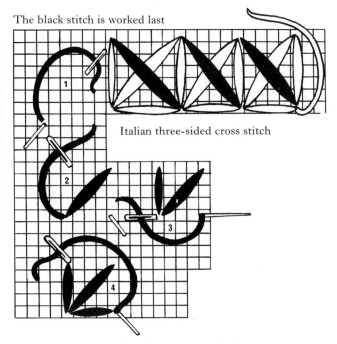

Italian three-sided cross stitch

168   Method of working Italian three-sided stitch

169   Alternating cushion stitch: a variation of cushion stitch

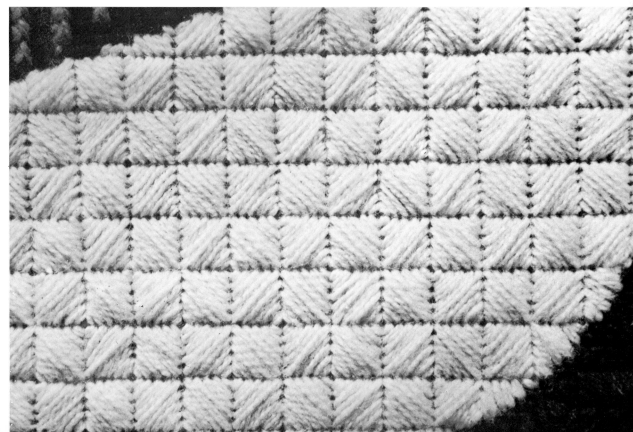

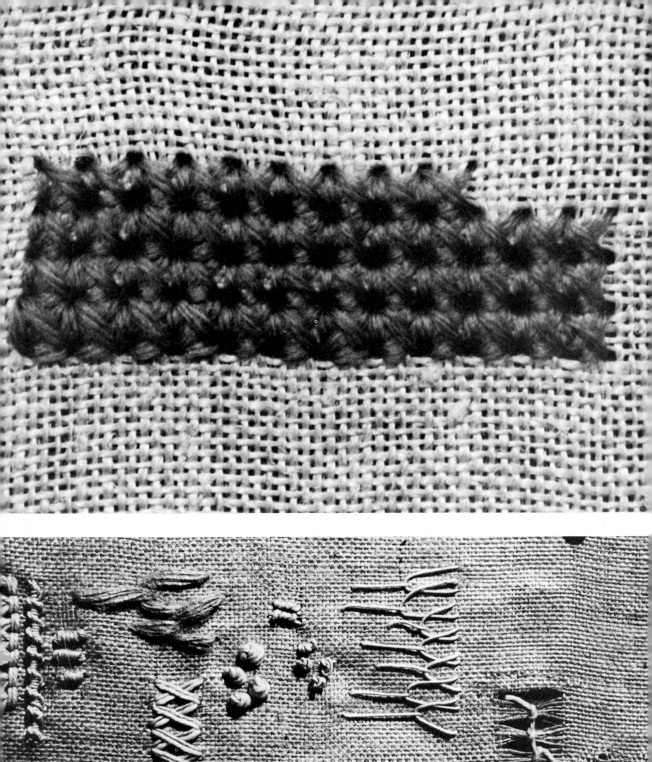

172 Satin stitch. Large blocks of satin stitch worked with tent stitch gives an interesting textural effect

Opposite
170 Three-sided Italian stitch worked on flax canvas. The appearance of this stitch is completely different when worked on this more flexible type of canvas owing to its pulling qualities

171 Stitches worked in string with an example of how the more flexible canvases appear when fringed

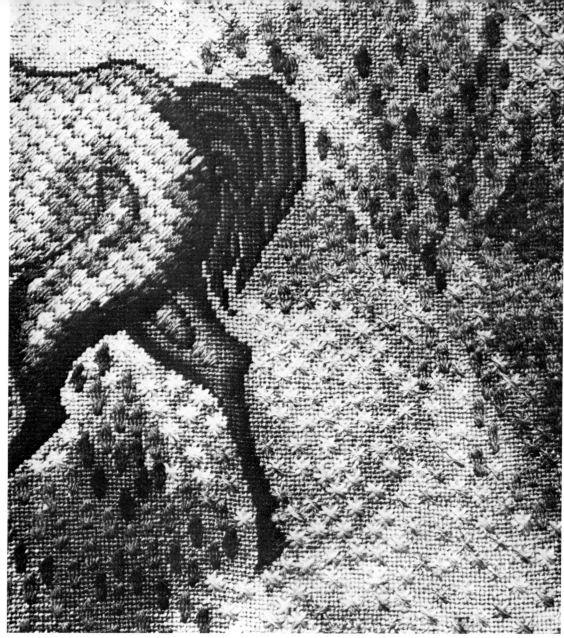

173 Smyrna stitch dotted all over a shaded background of tent stitch

174 Method of working Smyrna stitch

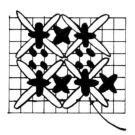

Smyrna, cross and tent stitches

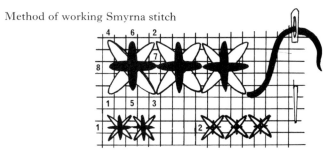

A tighter cross is formed by working over 2 threads instead of 4

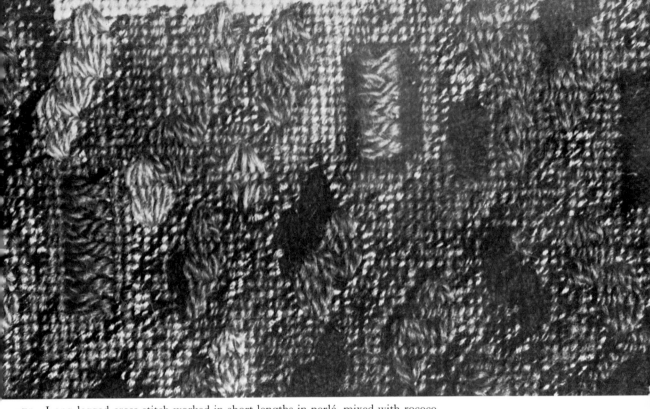

175 Long-legged cross stitch worked in short lengths in perlé, mixed with rococo stitch on a background of tent stitch

176 Wheatsheaf stitch and tent stitch on a background of rice stitch

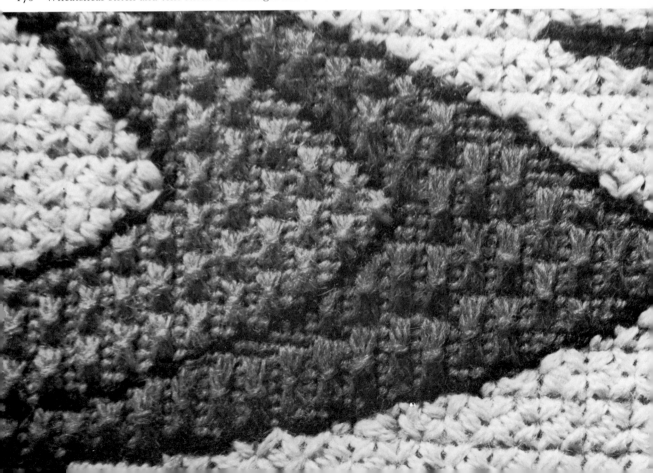

177 Wheatsheaf stitch worked diagonally, mixed with Smyrna and tent stitches with stem stitches at top left-hand corner

178 Method of working wheatsheaf stitch

Wheatsheaf

Wheatsheaf and tent using both thick and thin threads

179 *Red Goat*. A well-textured panel. Carpet thrums were used to work the back-ground, which is dark maroon, red and deep purple. Silk and cotton were also used
Lilian Hill

180 Detail of *Red Goat* showing Byzantine stitch on hind leg of goat

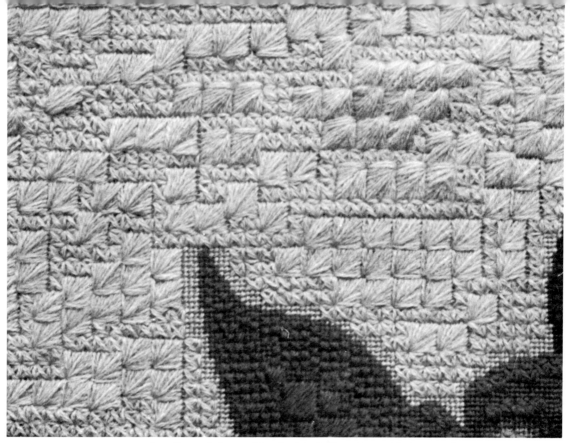

181 Fan stitch combined with Italian three-sided stitch. In the centre of the background, there is a section of fan stitch which has been worked from the opposite corner in order to give more variation to the texture

182 Long-legged cross stitch. Alternating rows of long-legged cross and Smyrna stitches

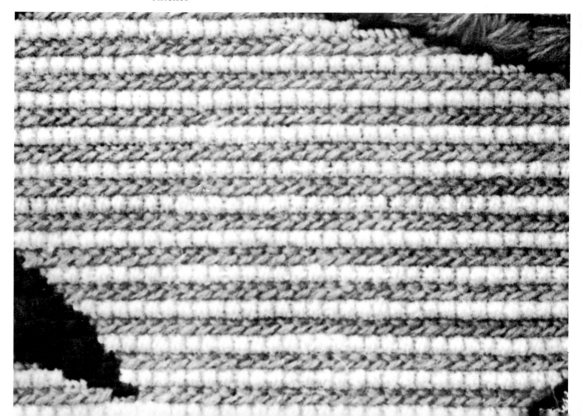

183 Eyelet stitch. A very useful stitch which mixes well with other stitches

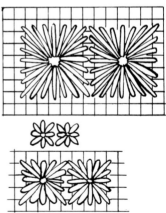

184 Method of working eyelet stitch

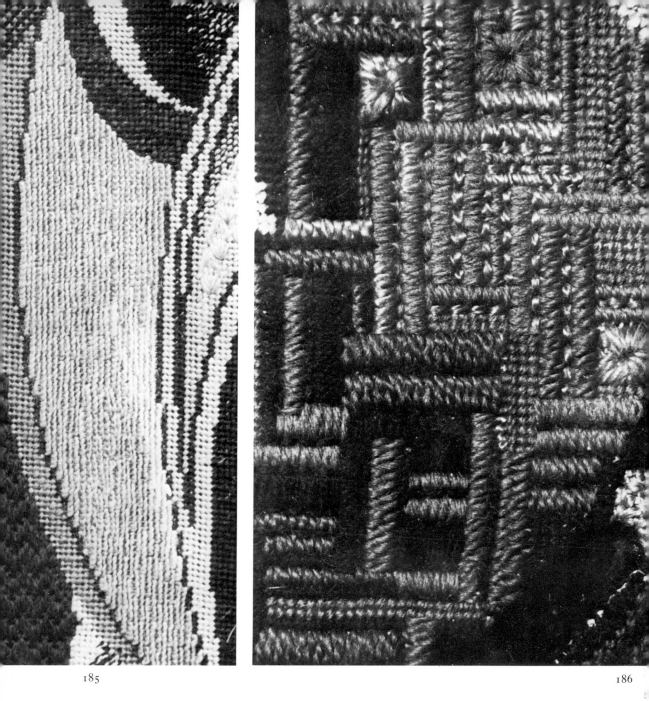

185 Buttonhole stitch. It is unusual to see this stitch worked on canvas. It is quite a useful stitch as it covers the threads of the canvas well, and it makes a welcome change to use this in place of the more common stitches when a change of stitch is required. The illustration shows the stitch worked over one thread of the canvas, but it could be worked over two or three threads with a slightly thicker thread to advantage

186 There are many different stitches which can be used together in order to give a very rich texture, such as short lengths of satin stitch combined with eyelet stitch, tent and back stitch

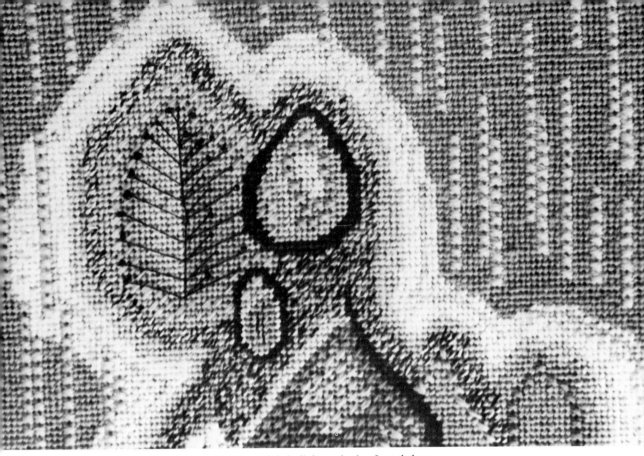

187 Varying lengths of cross stitch worked in a slightly lighter shade of wool than
the tent-stitch background

188 Cross stitch, long-legged cross stitch with flecked tent stitch

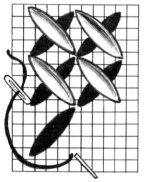

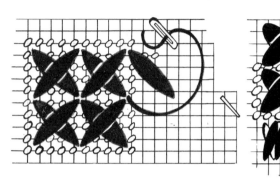

189   Method of working cross stitch

Like tent stitch, cross stitch can be
varied in order to get unusual results

190   Cross stitch worked diagonally

191 Tent stitch used to give a textural effect with plenty of movement

192 Tent stitch. This is a very clever way of shading with tent stitch in order to give an effect of atmosphere. It requires thought on the part of the embroiderer to achieve the change of tone required

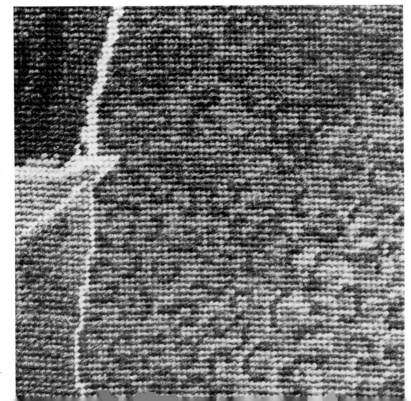

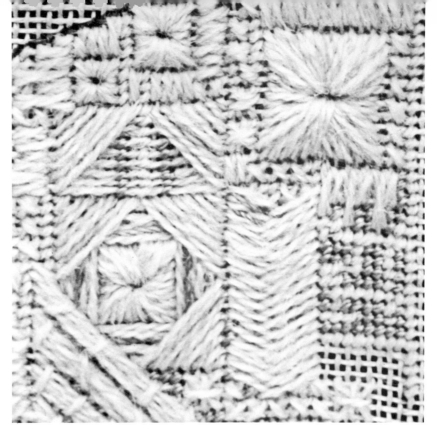

193 Straight stitches used in conjunction with eyelets together with some couched threads

194 Cretan stitch. Similar to the previous illustration, but showing, at the bottom left-hand side of the photograph a short length of cretan stitch, and at the bottom are some straight stitches worked in uneven lengths

195   *Foxes*. The design for this panel was taken from a Christmas card, and adapted for working on canvas
                                                                    Louise Beardow

196   *Foxes* detail. Smyrna and tent stitch together gives a wonderful embroidered representation of the surface of the back of this fox

197 Ghiordes or Turkish knot together with eyelet and satin stitches

198 Gold kid, gold purl, creosoted string, wool and silk were all used quite success-fully in working this panel in a free treatment of stitches

199 Detail of table lamp base. Victorian jet beads used with deep-coloured ▶ iridescent jewels and a free use of stitches help to give this piece of work a remarkable richness of texture

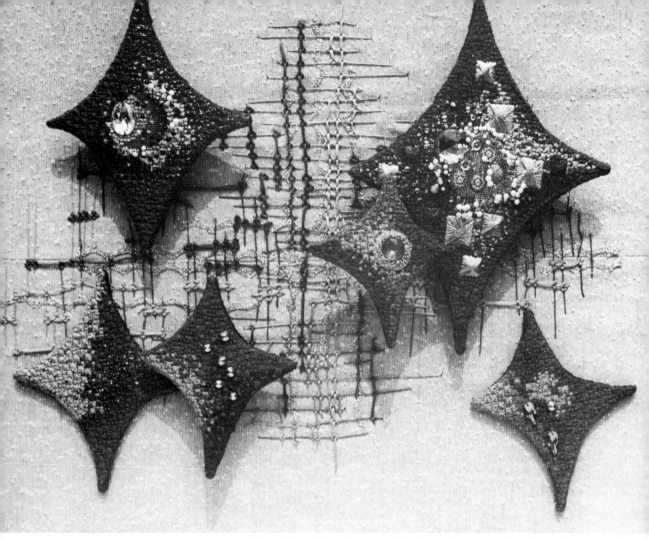

200 Pincushion. The shapes on this three-dimensional panel are first worked on canvas, cut out and fixed at varying distances from the backboard which is covered with furnishing material, embroidered. The size of the panel is 19 in. × 27 in.

Miriam Bawden

Opposite
201 Details of pincushion. There are two motifs only on this panel which are padded in the centre to accommodate the pins

5 Transferring designs to canvas

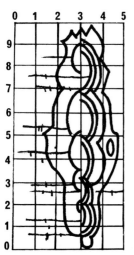

0 1 2 3 4 5

9
8
7
6
5
4
3
2
1
0

202 Method of enlarging a small ink blot

Enlarging a design

To enlarge a small drawing in preparation for working on canvas enclose it within a square or rectangle which is itself then divided into a grid of smaller squares. The actual size of the squares in the grid will naturally depend upon the size of the drawing to be enlarged, but they might possibly vary from $\frac{1}{4}$ in. to 1 in. The construction of the grid should be done by first drawing a vertical and a horizontal centre-line and working outwards from them to the edges in each direction. If the drawing to be enlarged must not be marked, a tracing of it should first be made, and then the grid of squares can be drawn upon the tracing. The lines of the grid should be numbered, starting at the bottom left-hand corner of the grid with nought and numbering both vertically and horizontally. It must next be decided by how many times the original drawing is to be enlarged, and then on another sheet of paper a square or rectangle must be drawn that same amount larger than the original square or rectangle. This new square or rectangle must be divided up into a grid containing exactly the same number of squares as the original one. Upon this new grid a free-hand drawing may be made by matching the lines on the drawing with their position on the original grid.

Tracing

When a design has been finished and drawn up on paper, it should be outlined with black paint, Indian ink or a fine felt-nib pen. The outline must be dark and thick enough to enable the design to be clearly seen when the canvas upon which it is to be worked is placed over it. The canvas chosen must have the appropriate size of mesh for the design: it must be just coarse enough to enable the design to be worked easily, but it should be remembered that there is no advantage in using a canvas with too fine a mesh, as this simply means working an unnecessary number of stitches to the inch.

The next step is to mark in the centre lines, both vertically and horizontally, on the canvas as well as on the paper design. The design should then be pinned on to a drawing-board and the canvas placed on top of it. The centre of the canvas should be fixed with a drawing-pin to the exact centre of the design and the centre lines on the canvas carefully matched to the centre-lines of the design and pinned down in this position. The rest of the canvas should then be eased out with the hand from the centre outwards and pinned down securely all round with drawing-pins. The design is now ready for tracing.

If the drawing-board is now tilted up against a table with the light coming from behind the person who is going to trace the design, the latter should be clearly discernible through the mesh of the canvas. Should it, however, be difficult to see the outline of the design, shading the canvas with the left hand against light coming from above will often help considerably to make the line stand out more clearly. This outline should now be carefully traced on to the canvas. For this purpose some people use black oil paint and others Indian ink, but I prefer always to use black water-colour paint. Oil paint, I find, dries too hard and shiny, and Indian ink tends to run so that the line becomes thick and blurred. One should use the paint on the dry side and keep the traced line as fine and dark as possible. I find that a number five sable hair brush is the most useful size of brush for tracing, but, if the design is very simple and uncomplicated, a fine felt-nib pen can be used. The brush or pen should be held in an upright position and used with a slightly scrubbing motion. It will take a little time to get used to tracing on to canvas, but with care and patience a reasonable result can be achieved.

The principal thing to concentrate on whilst tracing is to keep closely to the line of the design. Sometimes, however, it becomes necessary when tracing to make slight adjustments to a design. An experienced canvas-work designer will automatically bear in mind the limiting nature of the square mesh and will design accordingly, but to a beginner these limitations are not always apparent at the design stage, but become noticeable during the tracing, when corrections can be made directly on to the canvas. The main thing to watch for and to avoid is the line which comes just off the straight of the canvas thread. This line should, if possible, be made to run either straight on the canvas thread or at a definite angle to it. It is best in any case to avoid using very small shallow curves in canvas-work design.

203   The outlined design in place under the canvas and being pinned in position at the centre lines

204   Design being traced on to canvas with the hand shading the design, to enable the outline design to be seen more clearly. It also gives the correct upright position of the brush

205 Canvas with tracing partly worked

Method of working on canvas

When working on canvas, it is important to use a tapestry needle, the
eye of which must be large enough to take the wool easily without rubbing
the thread. The length of the piece of wool in the needle should not
exceed 15 in.; otherwise the wool may fray during the working. Ideally
each length of wool should be held before use in one hand and be pulled
through between the first finger and thumb-nail of the other hand in
order to free it from all surplus fluff, which might clog the hole in the
canvas and so weaken the wool as to cause it to break. It is always best to
start work by passing the thread through the canvas from above with a
knot at the end of the wool to prevent the end from passing right through,
and to do this a short distance from the desired starting-point in the
design, so that the end of the working thread will be caught in on the
underside of the canvas and will then be covered up by subsequent work.
Afterwards the knot on the surface can be cut off. Each length of wool
should be finished off in a similar way by bringing up the end of the thread
to the front of the canvas at a distance from the last stitch worked, and by
cutting this end off as soon as the length of thread under the canvas has
been caught in by subsequent stitches. By keeping the knots and ends
of the wool on the surface of the work, the embroiderer leaves the back
of the work free from obstruction, and this enables the needle to have
easy access to the holes in the canvas. After one has been working for
some time, it may happen that the ply of the wool becomes untwisted,

and, as a result, the wool breaks. In order to prevent this from happening, a half twist of the needle should be made every so often in the same direction as the ply of the wool has been twisted. If more than one thread is used in the needle, care must be taken that these threads do not become twisted around one another, as this will make the finished work look uneven.

When everything is ready to begin a piece of canvas work, the worker is well advised to start with some part of the design and not with the background, or at least not to work the background until the outline of the design has been worked. This obviates the possibility of encroaching on to some threads of canvas which are needed for working the design. It should be remembered that, although a wrongly placed stitch can be rectified by working over it with the correct one, only wool will generally cover up both silk and wool successfully and silk, when worked over wool, will seldom cover the under stitch. One should never be afraid to unpick any section of the work which appears to be wrong. Designing does not in fact end when the initial drawing is completed, but continues throughout the working. Often it becomes apparent in the working that a colour or tone is wrong and must be altered, or sometimes it may be necessary to

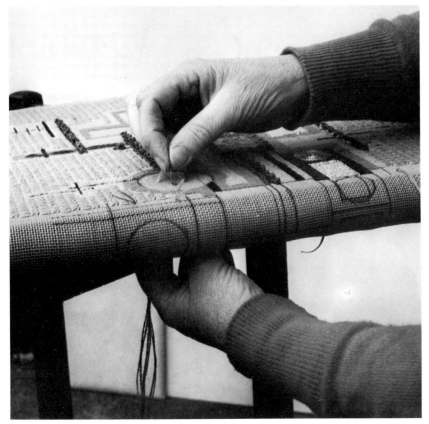

206 Method of working. One hand on top of the work, whilst the other hand remains underneath the frame

add or omit a line or to lighten or darken a shade. It is also necessary to remember, when working a shaded shape, that, if a dark effect is wanted, then the darkest area should be worked first, and if a light effect is needed, then the silk highlight and the pale shades should be worked first. This effect arises because the nature of the basic material and the type of stitch used in canvas work tend to lead a worker slightly to extend the area he has set out to work in a certain shade and, therefore, to leave less space in the remainder of the given shape for subsequent shades.

It is seldom possible or desirable to complete a piece of work exactly as planned, and creative thought must go on throughout the entire execution of the work; consideration must be given very carefully to every change of stitch and colour, for without this careful deliberation the finished embroidery can become only partially successful and may lack just that little extra element which makes the final result both interesting and lively. One of the greatest dangers is that the worker may get too close to the work and become too involved with the detail of small areas without keeping in mind the requirements of the design as a whole. It is, therefore, very necessary from time to time during the working to place the piece of work in a prominent position in a room and to leave it there for a day or two in order to have the opportunity of studying it from a distance and from all angles and of deciding on the further course of the work.

During the actual working the frame upon which the work is stretched should be correctly positioned. The screw-bar type of frame has its own floor stand and therefore presents no problems, but, if a floor stand is not available, or, if the flat-bar type of frame is being used, the frame can be supported between the worker and the edge of a table, or, better still, be placed flat and be supported between the edges of two tables or between two trestles. This latter method, like the use of a screw-bar frame on a floor stand, frees both hands for the actual working. One hand can then be kept on top of the work whilst the other remains underneath the canvas, a method of proceeding which not only makes for a very even finish, but also enables a greater speed to be achieved. It does take a little time to become accustomed to working in this way with one hand above and one below the canvas, but the improvement in the quality of the finished work makes it well worth while to persevere.

Beads, jewels, tree bark and any other objects which are sewn on to the surface of the canvas must be very firmly attached, so that there is no danger of their becoming loose and dropping off after a period of time.

It is never very pleasant having to unpick work, but, if this has to be done, it is quite easy to remove a few lines of stitchery by picking back with the needle, but, if a large area has to be unpicked, it is easier to cut out the wool on the front of the work by slipping a needle under a line of stitches to raise them slightly from the canvas and cutting the stitches away from under the needle with a small, fine pair of scissors. Then the cut stitches may be pulled away from the back of the work. Care must be taken not to cut threads of the canvas during this process, but, if by mischance this is done, the damage can be repaired by withdrawing a thread of canvas from the edge of the work and threading it into the place of the cut thread. To do this put a knot in the end of the new canvas thread, and with a needle take it through the canvas from the front of the work to the back a short distance from the damaged part. If the canvas is already worked, slip the needle through the worked stitches so that it emerges near the cut thread and work the new thread into the canvas to replace the damaged one. On the other side of the damaged area the new thread can again be carried through the worked stitches and brought up to the front of the work. If the area around the cut thread is unworked, then the new thread must be darned through the canvas for approximately 1 in. on each side of the break. The ends of the cut thread should then be pulled to the back of the work. When the new thread of canvas has finally been worked over again, the loose end of the thread and the knot at the other end can be cut off.

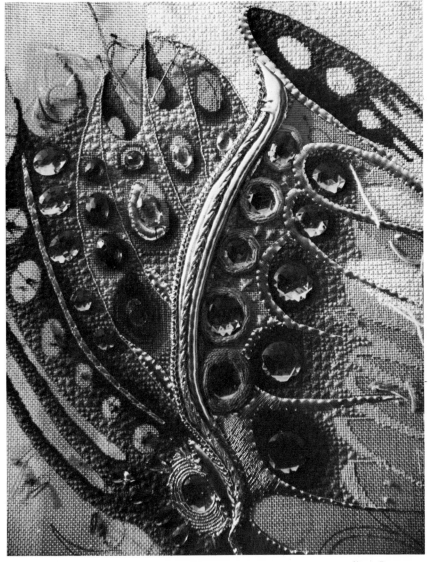

207   *Golden wings* Detail of panel when partly worked   *Joan Lawrance*

Opposite
208 Detail of *Golden Wings*. Method employed in attaching the jewels on to the canvas

209 Another detail of the same panel. A different way of mounting a jewel or other items. These should be helped in some way to integrate into their backgrounds and not be allowed just to sit on the surface of the canvas

210   Detail of *Blue Glass* panel. Jewel in an acorn cup setting formed from button-holing into a square of back stitches

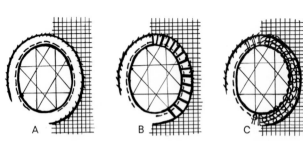
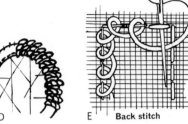

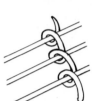

E Back stitch

211   Fixing jewels. The jewel is surrounded by a ring of
felt

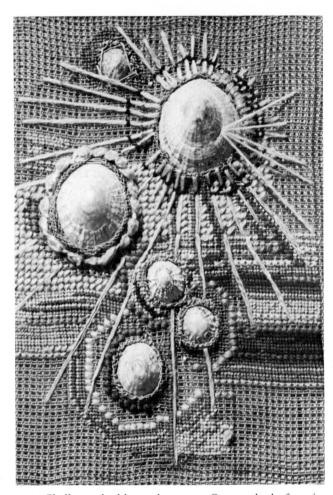

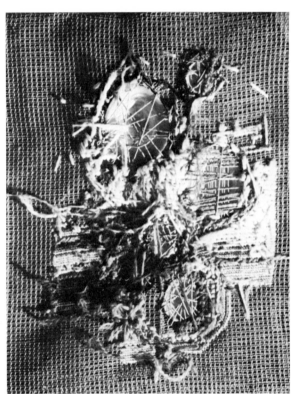

213   Reverse side of 212

212   Shells on double-mesh canvas. One method of sewing shells on to canvas.
Holes are cut in the canvas slightly smaller than the shells, which are inserted from the
back of the canvas. The cut edge of canvas is folded under to make a neat edge and
the shells are held in position by threads taken across the back of the work, as shown in
the accompanying photograph

214 *Elizabeth Desmoulins*

214 A partly worked panel showing knots on the surface holding the ends of new threads. When a new piece of thread is commenced, always knot it at the end and take the needle through to the back of the work, bring the needle up through the hole where work is to commence. Leave the knot on the surface until it is worked over at the back, when it will be safe to cut it off

215 Three small pieces of tree bark stitched firmly on to the background and surrounded by stitches and by bouclé wool couched at intervals. It is a useful exercise to allow a small design like this to evolve gradually on the canvas without any preconceived ideas, as it allows great freedom for the use of different materials and techniques

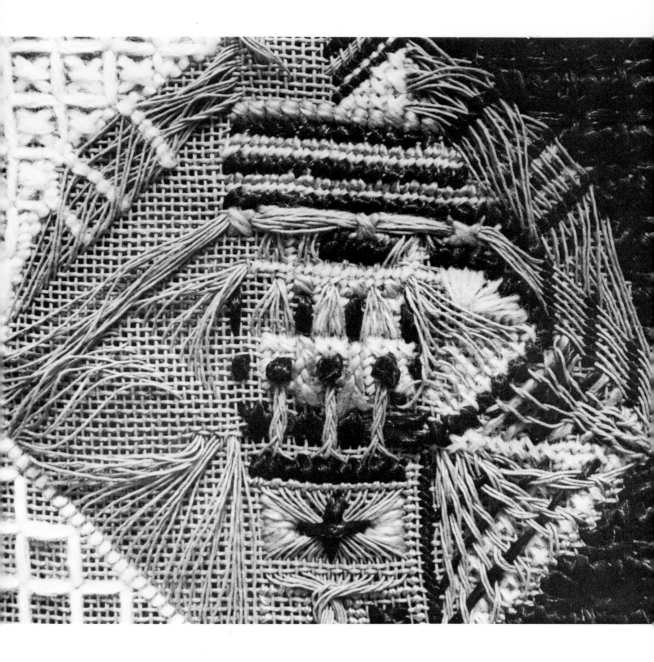

216 Free designing on canvas. A spare piece of canvas was frayed and the warp threads were removed to leave the weft threads attached to the selvedge. These threads were then brought through the holes in another piece of canvas on to the front and worked, plaited or caught down with stitches, no previous design having been prepared. This is a completely free way of designing in which, by twisting, plaiting and couching down different thicknesses of thread, very interesting results can be achieved. This particular piece has one part of the background worked in black raffene and the other part in white wool

217

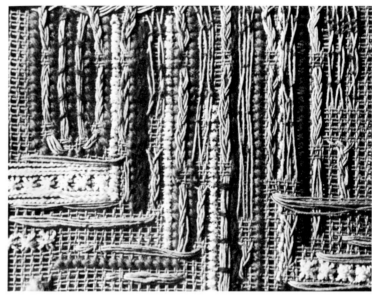

218

219

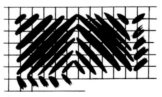

Alternating cushion stitch

Each square takes 5 slanting flat
stitches starting with a tent stitch
Each square is worked alternately
from left to right

Opposite

217 A free treatment of stitchery using soft embroidery cotton, perlé and perlita yarn

218 Another piece of free designing, using canvas threads, knitting cotton and perlé worked on Penelope canvas

219 Threads of the canvas are here used in working a design together with wool and other fibres

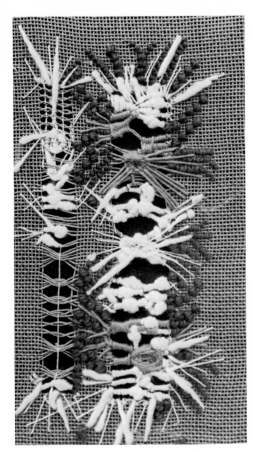

220 Free designing in which warp threads are withdrawn from the canvas and very free needle weaving is worked with slub-weaving yarn and thick cotton. This thick cotton is also used for the additional stitchery

221 Further free designing. A length of Winchester-type canvas is fringed and honeycombed. It is partly folded and applied on to congress canvas. Stitches are worked with threads of the flax canvas. The varying shades of the two types of canvas make a very pleasing contrast

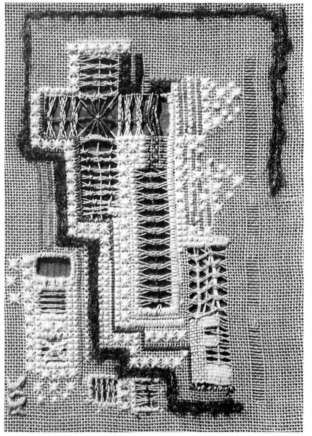

222

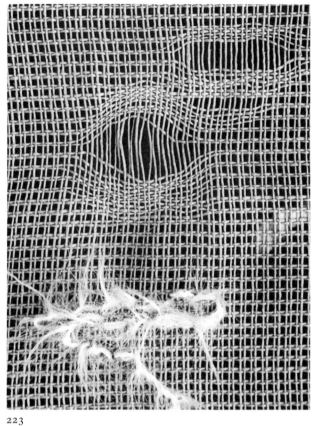

223

224

142

Opposite

222   An unfinished piece of canvas work, showing areas of drawn-thread work. Many warp threads could also be withdrawn over a large area and coloured threads could be used to replace them, thus altering the foundation material, or needle weaving could be used together with a variety of stitches

223   Threads displaced in preparation for working needle weaving or other free treatments

224   A bunch of threads laid down at random is caught down with long horizontal stitches in Rya wool. Mixed lines of eyelet, satin, tent and knotted stitches are worked in orderly disarray. The knotted stitch used is the Ghiordes knot which is used in Turkey work

225   Bird abstract worked in a variety of stitches, giving a bold, strongly textured effect. The colouring is black, grey, gold and white   *Louise Beardow*

Templates or patterns

To take the template or pattern of a stool top place it upside down in the centre of a large sheet of paper. First draw on the paper all round the stool with a pencil pressed against the side of the stool top. This will give the sight-line or, in other words, the area in which the main part of the design will be contained. Then fold up the paper around the sides of the stool and, with the pencil laid flat on the underside of the framework of the stool, draw a line all round on the folded-up surface of the paper. This gives the 'drop' or 'turn down' area, which is usually between 2 and 3 in. deep. The same process is used for taking templates of chair-seat squabs. For fully upholstered chair seats place the paper over the seat and mark all round the edge with a pencil. Then fold the paper in half from back to front of the seat. If the two halves of the seat are not symmetrical, as will be revealed when the paper template is thus folded, it is probably due to the fact that the upholstery is slightly uneven. It should always be assumed that the framework of the chair is itself symmetrical, and the template should, therefore, be corrected by splitting any difference in outline between the two halves of the seat.

Church kneelers

Church kneelers vary in size according to the size of the area in which they will be placed. Small ones usually have a top measurement of approximately 12 in. × 9 in. with a 2 in. drop all round, but the average size is 14 in. × 10 in. with a 2 to 3 in. drop. For wedding ceremonies low upholstered stools are often thought more appropriate and more comfortable than traditional kneelers. These also vary in size according to the specific requirements of the church where they are to be used. In any case it is advisable to make contact with the individual church authorities before planning any article for use in a church.

Cushions

Canvas embroidery is ideally suited for covering cushions, but owing to its long life great care must be exercised in preparing the designs. Some years ago the usual size for a cushion was 24 in. square, but now they have diminished somewhat in size, and cushions of 20 in. or smaller appear to be popular. They can, of course, be of any shape, circular, square, crescent or pillow-shaped. A design which can be viewed equally well from all angles is usually desirable, and this applies not only to cushions, but also to rugs and stool tops.

Evening bags

Worked on canvas, evening bags can be very beautiful, particularly when the background is worked in a neutral or light shade of silk. The design can then be worked in wool and silk with gold and silver threads together with jewels or beads. These bags can be made in various shapes and sizes. If it is decided to use a metal top, it is better to purchase this first and then to cut a pattern of a size and shape suitable for it. It is necessary to work a 1 in. gusset, the length of which has to be measured from the top edge of the metal frame on one side, and not from the lower edge, as might be expected, right round the base of the bag to the top of the metal frame on the other side. This extra length of gusset is apparently needed when the bag is to be made up professionally.

Table lamps

Canvas embroidery can be successfully used to cover the base of a table lamp. As a foundation for the work obtain either a length of asbestos piping $4\frac{1}{2}$ to 5 in. in diameter, which can be purchased from a builders' merchant, or a very thick and strong cardboard tube of the same diameter. Cut off a length of 12 to 14 in. from the pipe or tube and obtain two circular pieces of wood of the same diameter, which can then be fitted into the openings at each end of the tube. A hole is now bored through the top piece of wood for the attachment of the lamp socket. From this socket the flex is taken down through the tube and out through a hole bored near the base of the tube. The second circular piece of wood is then fixed in position at the base. A rectangular piece of canvas, which exactly fits round the tube, is then worked for the covering. The design should be kept simple, and it should be remembered that only a very small portion of the design will be seen at any one time. The top piece of wood can be covered with canvas work or with gold leather, and the base will need to be covered with felt. See figures 260–2.

Mirrors

Embroidered mirror surrounds have been popular in this country since Stuart times. Then they were embroidered in silk on silk material, but later they were worked on canvas, and canvas-embroidered surrounds are still popular today.

In designing mirror surrounds for canvas work it is desirable to keep to simple shapes, otherwise difficulties may be encountered when it comes to mounting the finished work. A rectangular shape is naturally the easiest to work and to mount, but a curved top can be used, as also a circular aperture in the middle. There will be little difficulty in working the latter, but it may present some slight problem in mounting.

6 Materials and equipment

Frames

Frames for use in canvas work must be strong as they have to take very great strain from the tense canvas. Two types which are suitable for this work are the Dryad, or flat-bar type, and the screw-bar type. The flat-bar frame is the most suitable for use with large canvases, as it is particularly strong and remains quite rigid under strain. This type of frame also possesses the advantage that the canvas on it can be rolled up to leave an area for working which is smaller than can be obtained on the screw-bar frame.

The flat-bar frame consists of two rollers, one across the top and one across the bottom of the frame, and two strong flat pieces of wood as side-pieces with holes at intervals in them to take split pins or wooden pegs. The ends of these side-pieces are passed through large slots in the ends of the two rollers and fixed in position with the split pins or wooden pegs. This type of frame is quite easy and cheap to make, and I have seen many home-made ones with rollers made from broom handles, which have proved quite satisfactory. Suitable split pins can be obtained from any cycle or car supplies shop.

In order to attach the canvas to such a frame, it is necessary to fix tape or webbing $1\frac{1}{2}$ in. wide along the length of each roller by means of tintacks at 1 in. intervals and to mark the centre point very carefully on each of these pieces of tape or webbing. The centre point on one edge of the canvas is placed exactly at the centre point of one of the lengths of webbing and the two are stitched together. The selvedge of the webbing and the selvedge of the canvas (or the cut edge of the canvas which has been turned down half an inch) should be placed edges together and oversewn two threads only of the canvas and a corresponding amount of the webbing selvedge so that a butt joint is made. Starting at the centre point and pulling both canvas and webbing edges taut, overcast with a strong thread from the centre outwards, fastening off very securely at the ends, as otherwise the strain of the stretched canvas may pull the stitching apart. This procedure should be repeated in order to attach the opposite edge of the canvas to the other roller. The canvas may now be rolled up to a convenient size and the side-pieces slotted into the rollers. If one roller is then fixed by means of the split pins or pegs, the canvas may be made taut by pulling on the opposite roller and fixing it in a similar way on its side. The canvas is now extended top and bottom, and in order to extend it sideways a length of webbing or any other strong material must be back-stitched along the sides of the canvas. These side strips of material must be sewn on after the canvas has been rolled up to the required size and is stretched, as in no case must the side-pieces of webbing be wound round the rollers, because this would cause the edges of the canvas to become tight whilst the centre of the canvas remained slack and would make it more difficult to work. Finally with a packing needle or a very

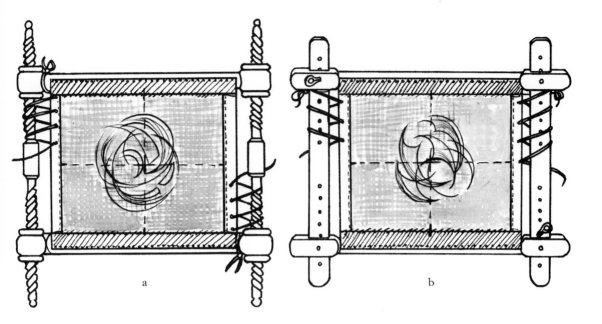

226a Screw-bar frame

226b Dryad type or flat-bar frame

strong, large-eyed tapestry needle and some strong, fine string lace through the webbing and over the side-pieces of the frame at about 1 in. intervals and fasten off securely. The canvas is now ready for working.

If a screw-bar frame is to be used, the main difference to be noted is that the side elements of the frame, which fit into the rollers at top and bottom, are round instead of flat and have a screw thread at each end. These side bars pass through holes at the ends of the rollers and are held in position by circular wooden screw rings. The fitting of the canvas to the frame is similar to the process with the flat-bar frame, except that the canvas is stretched taut by tightening the screw rings. (See figure 227.) When the canvas has been stretched sufficiently taut, a second ring is screwed on and tightened against the first one in order to hold the roller firm at each end. (See figure 226a.)

The simplest of all frames is the one illustrated in figure 228. It is a simple rectangular frame made from $2\frac{1}{2}$ in. $\times$ $1\frac{3}{4}$ in. battens, which are nailed together at the corners, and can easily be made at home. This is quite a strong type of frame to work on, but the disadvantage of using it is that such a frame must be large enough to take the fully extended canvas, as it is not possible to roll up the canvas as on the other types of frame. The canvas must be fixed to the frame all round either with drawing-pins or with tintacks, and it is thus only suitable for working comparatively small pieces of work.

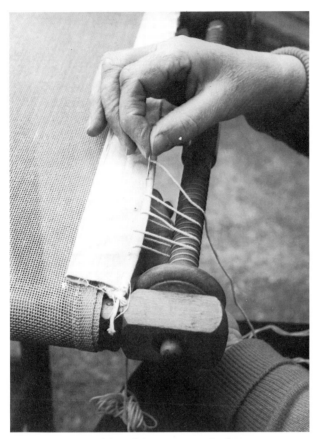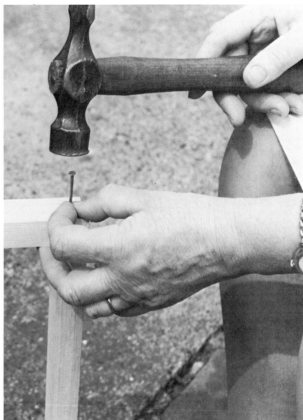

227 Lacing the sides of the canvas to the frame   228 Making the simplest of all frames

Canvas

Canvas is made of linen, hemp, cotton or gauze (for use in making small, fine articles, such as evening bags) and it is either of single or double mesh, the latter being sometimes called Penelope canvas. The number of the mesh indicates the number of threads to the inch. Suitable meshes for chair seats, stools, etc, are usually 18, 16 or 14 threads to the inch. I consider that 16 mesh is the best size to use, but some people prefer to work on the finer 18 mesh. Single-mesh canvas is preferable to double mesh, because all stitches can be worked on it without difficulty, and, as tent stitch is a main basic stitch, which is used considerably in most pieces of work, the use of double-mesh canvas would often entail splitting the threads in order to work this stitch.

The best-quality canvas should always be used, if possible linen canvas, which is obtainable from France, Denmark and elsewhere on the Continent, but unfortunately no longer obtainable in this country. The best canvas obtainable here is a polished cotton thread, made in widths of 27 in. or 36 in. in a natural colour. There are cheaper cotton canvases, both buff and white, which are stocked by most local stores, but these are very inferior in quality to the best and have a large amount of size used to stiffen them. It cannot be stressed too often that, because of the long life of canvas embroidery, only the very best materials should be used.

Some people prefer to use Winchester canvas, which is made from Italian hemp and is very flexible and strong. This canvas is particularly good for very large panels as it can be bought in widths of 50 in. and it is easier to join sections together than is the case with other stiffer types of canvas. Unfortunately Winchester canvas has recently ceased to be produced as a result of the failure of the hemp crop, and it may be discontinued permanently. As a replacement a very good canvas of a similar type, but made from flax, is being used and could become even more popular.

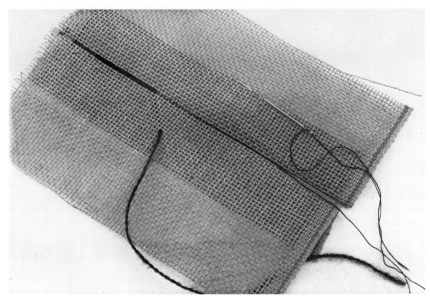

229   Joining canvas

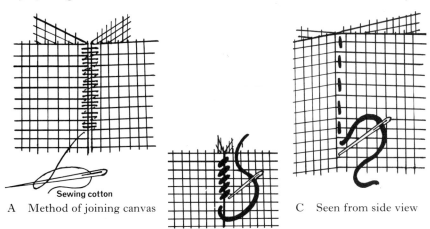

A   Method of joining canvas

B   To work tent stitch after joining

C   Seen from side view

230   Method of joining canvas

Good-quality hessian, which is made from hemp and jute, can also be used as a basis for certain types of canvas work, providing it is of a fairly tight, firm weave, and it could be used to an extent to replace Winchester canvas. It is reasonably strong, can be bought in both wide and narrow widths and can be very useful for working modern free types of design. Hessian is very pliable and can be worked with all the usual canvas stitches. In addition it can be made to do many unusual and exciting things which would be impossible with ordinary canvas: it can be fringed, frayed or pulled, and threads can be withdrawn, all of which can help to give interesting and pleasing effects.

Canvases of a loose, flexible weave, such as Winchester canvas and hessian, give a slightly different appearance to the worked stitches as compared with the effect obtained on the usual polished thread canvas, which is a more rigid material. Most designs using so-called canvas stitches, when worked on these more flexible materials, take on the look of seventeenth- and eighteenth-century canvas embroideries, which were worked on a linen thread material similar to the kind now used for pulled work. Stitches, such as eyelet, diagonal, Hungarian and rococo, which have a certain pulling tendency, are shown to especially good effect on the Winchester type of canvas, because this material allows small perforations to appear between stitches, and the latter add much to the appearance of the finished work.

231 Drawing lines on the canvas as a guide before tacking the final corner

232 Stretching and tacking down the final corner of the canvas. This may require the use of a pair of upholsterer's stretchers

Wools, silks, etc

For working on canvas such things as chair seats and all other upholstered and free-standing articles wool is the principal material used, as it is easy to work with, is strong and covers the canvas threads well. It is also extremely durable and has the advantage of wearing clean.

A two-ply Shetland wool, or any other similar type of wool, is suitable for this work. Atherstone wool can also be used; it is harder and more tightly spun and is rather less hairy than the Shetland wool. Both of these types of wool in white are suitable for dyeing with natural dyes, but the Atherstone wool requires greater quantities of dyestuff owing to its tighter twist. Skeins of crewel wool and Appleton wool are good, but these wools have to be used double on any canvas coarser than 18 mesh. Finally, many knitting wools can be used, provided that they are reasonably strong and are not too hairy.

Four-ply tapestry wool is only suitable for use with 16 mesh or coarser canvases, but it can be used on canvas of a finer mesh, if it is split in two, provided that the twist is put back into it again.

Silk is quite suitable for using on canvas: it is used mainly for working highlights in a design or for the background in small articles such as evening bags, table-lamp bases, mirror surrounds, jewel boxes, etc.

Now that production of Filoselle silk, which is a stranded silk, has been discontinued, probably the best type to use is Silk Embroidery Twist, which is a two-ply silk sold in skeins. Filo Floss is still obtainable, but this silk is somewhat difficult to use on canvas, as it is very loosely spun and is inclined to catch and cling to everything. Pure silk buttonhole twist, sold on paper spools at most of the large stores, is also very useful. There are two thicknesses of this silk: the thicker one would have to be used double on all canvases coarser than 18 mesh, and the thinner one, which, besides being very suitable for mixing with wool to give certain speckling effects, can also be used for highlights, would have to be used for this purpose with at least four strands in the needle.

Stranded cottons, perlé, coton-à-broder and many other types of cotton, linen and rayon threads are also used on canvas, but, if it is a question of choice between cotton and silk for working either backgrounds or highlights, I would always prefer silk, as cotton lacks the lustre of pure silk and can look very heavy and solid, if used for working large areas. Rayon in small quantities may be used, but it is rather a difficult material to work with, as the thread seems to take every opportunity of becoming twisted, and the worker is, therefore, obliged to untwist it after every few stitches, with the inevitable result that the process of the work is impeded.

For working wall-panels and pictures there is an unlimited choice of materials: in addition to the usual types of wool mentioned above, it is possible to use Bernat Klein wools, lurex, thrums, raffene, gold, silver and other metal threads, cotton—including crochet cottons—all types of string, weaving yarns, perlé and the various types of silk thread. It is always worth while to keep an eye on the wool and thread counters in the shops in order gradually to build up a collection of interesting threads for future use from the wide variety of materials which are available today. Even threads which are too thick for the particular mesh of canvas can be used by couching them down on the surface.

151

In this connection, too, a useful collection can be made of all types of sequins and beads, pieces of mirror glass, stained glass or glass which has been melted down in a kiln—even scraps of waste glass material from glass-blowing factories—together with any other kind of found object which appeals to the finder as suitable for this work.

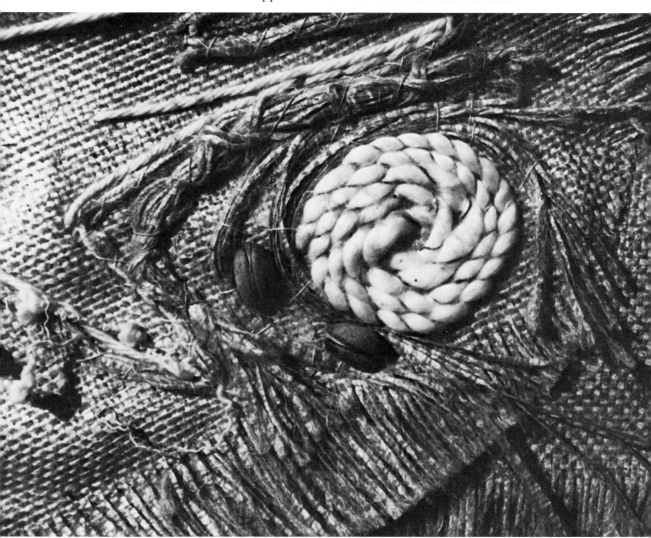

233   Good-quality hessian used in place of Winchester canvas for working free-style panels. This material is not, however, recommended for chair seats or stool tops

Opposite
234   Detail of large panel worked on hessian in bouclé, weaving yarns and threads of hessian couched down

235   Hessian panel, showing various fringed effects. Winchester-type canvas would give an even better result

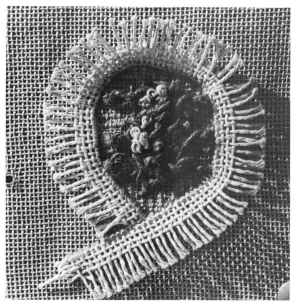

236

237

238

239 Another suggestion for fringing

Opposite
236 Fringed Motif. A circular motif incorporating a fringed strip of canvas attached upon a background of canvas worked in the centre with creosoted string and white string in french knots

237 Fringed Motif. A 4 in. wide strip of canvas joined in a circle and fringed, has been attached upon a background of freely worked straight stitches to give a three-dimensional effect

238 Fringed and unfringed strips of canvas laid on the surface of the work are used in conjunction with canvas stitches

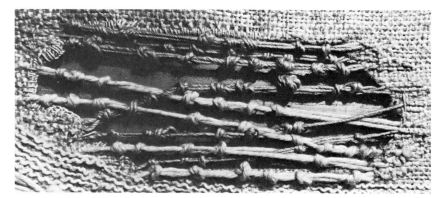

240   Detail of a panel. A hole has been cut in the canvas and knotted string inserted and partly surrounded with couched weaving yarns

241   Another detail showing how knitted twine has been used to form a case to hold a peach stone

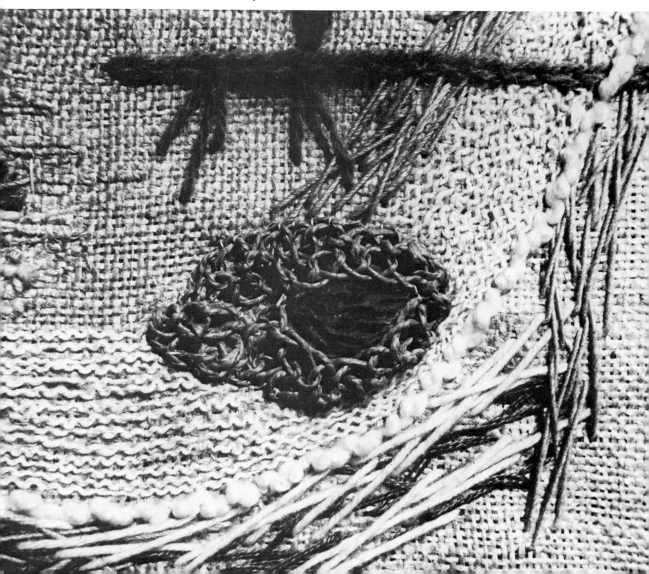

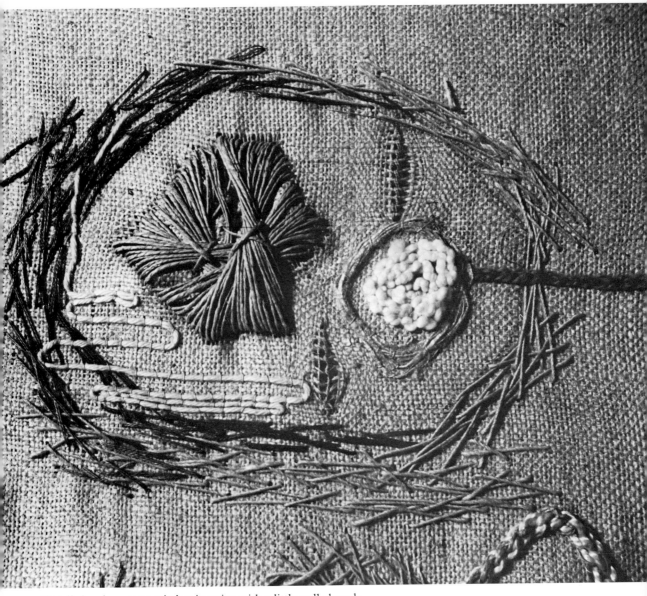

242　Detail showing coarse stitches in twine with a little pulled work

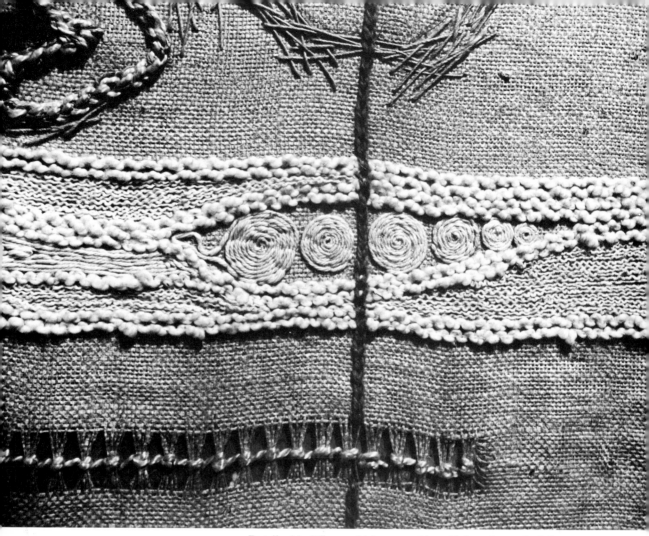

243 Detail with different thicknesses of bouclé threads couched down

244 Nylon raffene couched down with a knobbly weaving yarn. The piece is worked on Penelope canvas

245   Detail with wooden beads and coils of creosoted
string surrounded by antique purl

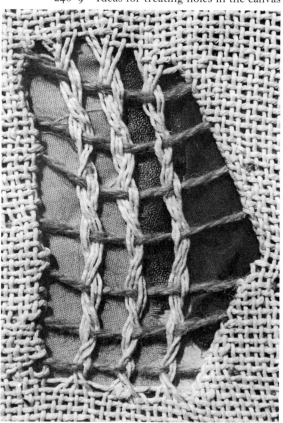

246 Knotted string

247 Threads withdrawn horizontally leaving the vertical threads to be twisted

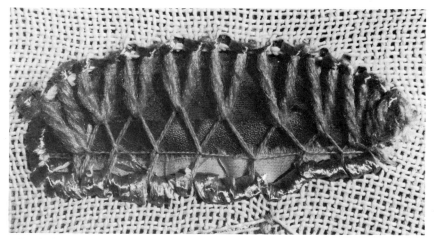

248 Coloured material placed behind a hole and laced over with wool of various thicknesses

249 A large hole has been cut in the canvas and strands of linen thread and thin string have been taken across it. Left of centre short lengths of thin string have been knotted and tied on to one of these cross threads. At the top, slightly right of centre, lengths of crocheted chain in wool have been used as a filling for a triangular shape formed by the cross threads

250 Detail of small abstract panel Galaxy. Coils of copper wire are stitched on to the canvas and strands of silk radiate from clusters of french knots

251 Further detail with twisted copper wire used in conjunction with canvas stitches

Needles

The needles used for working on canvas are called tapestry needles: they are large-eyed and blunt-ended and are obtainable in all sizes, the smaller the number, the coarser the needle. Numbers 18 and 20 are good useful sizes to have; number 14 is useful for grafting canvas or for using with carpet thrums, and number 26 should be used when two or three strands of silk are required. Packets of mixed sizes can be bought, but these packets contain mainly fine needles which are of little use other than for very fine mesh canvas or for working on gauze.

Scissors

A pair of finely pointed scissors is required, which is very necessary when unpicking has to be done.

Natural or vegetable dyeing

The results of dyeing with materials produced from natural sources are very rewarding, and the beauty and glowing warmth of colour obtained by these means well repay the amount of time and attention which need to be expended in the process. Many people are a little apprehensive about starting on this type of dyeing, but it is, in fact, very simple provided sufficient attention is given to accuracy in measuring out the dyes and getting the correct proportions between the various ingredients, and sufficient time and care is given to the actual process of dyeing.

There are really two processes involved in the dyeing of most colours: the first is called mordanting, and the second is the actual dyeing with dye-stuffs. Fastness of colour depends upon the mordanting, so this process is just as important as the dyeing itself. The word 'mordant', which is derived from the Latin *mordere*, meaning to bite, refers to any substances applied for the purpose of fixing a colour. This must be some ingredient which is capable of combining chemically with the dye-stuff being used, so as to set the colour and make it fast.

Great care must be taken during the mordanting process, firstly to see that the wool or other material to be dyed has been well washed and rinsed to remove all grease or other substance which might prevent the mordant taking properly, and secondly to allow enough time for the mordant to penetrate the fibre of the wool or other material thoroughly, because, if the process is hurried and superficial, the subsequent dyeing will be uneven and the colour will quickly fade. Furthermore, an unevenly mordanted skein of wool will never later dye evenly. Therefore the longer the time taken in the process and the greater the accuracy in weighing out the ingredients required, combined with thoroughness in the preliminary washing of the material to be dyed, the faster and more brilliant will be the final dyeing.

Substances most frequently used as mordants are the metallic salts of alum, chrome, tin and iron. Other ingredients, such as cream of tartar, although not themselves mordants, are used in conjunction with some of the mordants in order to brighten the colours. Great care must be taken to follow the quantities given in the recipes exactly, as too much alum will make the wool sticky and too much of the crystals of tin will make it brittle. The tin mordant is the only one I know which can completely ruin wool, and it is necessary to make sure that it is thoroughly dissolved before putting it into the dye bath, as a single undissolved grain of tin crystals touching a strand of wool will rot it. There is only one other process which I know in vegetable dyeing, where a mistake can render wool completely useless, and that is in dyeing with indigo. In the few cases where this has happened with indigo, and the wool has disintegrated and appeared as a slimy jelly, the trouble was probably due to an excessive use of caustic soda. Mistakes with other dye materials seem to leave the wool usable even if not quite the desired shade. This can always be re-dyed a darker shade or can be kept for future use.

Wool can be dyed immediately after mordanting or the mordanting and dyeing can even be done together in the same pot, but in the latter case the resulting colours are never so brilliant and vibrant.

Silk and wool require practically the same preparation, although high temperatures should never be used when dyeing silk. Wool is brought to the boil and simmered in the mordant for about one hour, but for silk it is better to keep the temperature down well below boiling point or to use a cold solution. Once the initial boiling of silk to get rid of the first casing of gum is completed, it is a case of silk boiled is silk spoiled.

The recipes given below are for small quantities of wool, which can be dyed quite easily at home in large enamelled saucepans. A suitable saucepan for this purpose should measure about 8 in. across the base and must be deep enough to take the wool easily when it is well covered with water. All saucepans used for dyeing should be kept solely for that purpose and must be perfectly clean and unchipped. For indigo dyeing a new enamelled saucepan or bowl is desirable and, if possible, this should be kept exclusively for indigo. If it has to be used for any other dye, it must first be thoroughly scoured out, otherwise it will cause the wool to become stained and marked. As a general rule it is best to use enamelled saucepans or bowls for all dyeing, but aluminium or iron saucepans or bowls can be used for certain colours: aluminium pans are suitable for bright colours, but iron ones should only be used for dark colours.

The skeins of wool for dyeing should be tied very loosely but securely in two or three places in order to prevent them from becoming entangled when in the dye bath. When the skeins have been well washed and rinsed thoroughly, they should be squeezed to remove all the excess water. Wool should never be twisted to remove water from it, as this may weaken it. The skeins of wool must always be entered into the mordant or dye bath in a damp state. Dry or partly dry wool will never dye evenly, and if mordanted wool has been allowed to dry out, it must be re-mordanted before being placed into the dye bath.

The principal mordants

Alum (potassium aluminium sulphate)
This is the most generally used of all the mordants and was known and used by dyers in ancient times in most parts of the world. In order to make the colour even and to brighten it, a proportion of cream of tartar (tartaric acid) should be added to the mordant bath.

Recipe for mordanting 1 lb of wool
4 oz alum
1 oz cream of tartar
These quantities are for coarse types of wool such as Shetland, Atherstone, etc. Use 3 oz of alum and a little less cream of tartar than in this recipe to mordant 1 lb of finer wool or to obtain paler shades.

Dissolve the alum and cream of tartar in a little water and add it to the pot of cold water in which the mordanting is to be done. There should be sufficient water comfortably to cover the wool. Gradually bring the temperature up and stir well. When the water begins to get warm, enter the damp wool and slowly bring the temperature up to boiling point. Then reduce the heat and let the wool simmer in the mordant for about one hour. Slightly less time might be given for finer wool. When the mordanting is finished, the pot should be removed from the heat and the wool lifted out with a glass rod or a clean stick, or, if preferred, it can be left in the pot to cool overnight. The excess water is then squeezed or pressed out by hand, but the wool must not be washed again at this stage.

While it is still damp, the mordanted wool may be immediately transferred to the dye bath, but it is better, if possible, to wrap it in a cloth and put this into a plastic bag so that it remains damp, and to leave it in a drawer or other dark place for four or five days. This makes sure that the mordant has thoroughly penetrated all the fibres. The wool must not be allowed to dry out during this time, as this would mean re-mordanting; if, however, it is found difficult to start the dyeing process after four to five days, the mordanted wool may be kept longer, provided it is still kept damp and in a dark place.

As the water evaporates from the pot during mordanting or dyeing, the wool should be removed from the solution and extra water added to bring the amount up to the original level. The solution should then be stirred well and the wool replaced to finish the process. The skeins of wool must be completely submerged during the whole operation and must always be removed from the pot before any extra water or other ingredient is added.

Chrome (bichromate of potash). This should be labelled POISON
Chrome is an excellent mordant for wool, leaving it soft to the touch, where other mordants are liable slightly to harden the wool. It is a comparatively modern mordant and was completely unknown to the dyer of 150 years ago. Its disadvantage is that, being very sensitive to light, it can cause uneven dyeing, if the wool is not completely submerged in the liquid, and it is, therefore, advisable to dye wool immediately after mordanting with chrome. If this is not always possible, the wool must be kept where all light is excluded from it. The cover must be kept on the pot all the time during mordanting and dyeing, and the wool must always be dried in the shade after the dyeing process has been completed. It should also be remembered that too much chrome impairs the colour and that the recipe must, therefore, be closely adhered to.

Recipe for mordanting 1 lb of wool
$\frac{1}{2}$ oz chrome
Dissolve the chrome in the pot of cold water and, whilst it is warming up, put in the thoroughly dampened wool. Cover the pot and gradually bring to the boil during the course of half an hour. Then reduce the heat and simmer for one hour, turning the wool over completely once or twice during that time, but taking great care to exclude as much light as possible and to replace the lid on the pot as promptly as possible. The wool should be washed well with soap and water after mordanting and it is then ready for dyeing.

Tin (stannous chloride, muriate of tin, tin crystals). This should be marked POISON
Tin can be used in two ways: it can be used as a mordant before dyeing, or it can be added to the dye bath towards the end of dyeing in order to brighten and intensify the colour. It is employed in the latter way mainly with cochineal, madder and some yellow dyes, when the wool or silk has been previously mordanted with alum, and bright shades are needed. The amount of tin crystals to be used to brighten these colours will depend on the shade required, and only a few crystals should be added at a time.

Recipe for mordanting 1 lb of wool
½ oz tin crystals
2 oz cream of tartar
When tin is used as a mordant before dyeing, the wool is entered into a cold mordant bath in which the tin crystals and cream of tartar have been thoroughly dissolved. Cream of tartar is nearly always used in conjunction with tin, but sometimes oxalic acid or nitric acid are used instead, and, when this is the case, the acids should always be completely dissolved in the bath before the dissolved tin crystals are added. The temperature is then raised to boiling point and kept at this point for an hour. The rest of the dyeing method is as for alum.

The following points should be borne carefully in mind. Acids should always be added to water and never water to acids. Whenever tin has been used, the wool should be washed in soapy water and rinsed well after dyeing. Tin crystals, like all other mordanting ingredients, must always be carefully dissolved before being added to the dye pot, and this is particularly the case if the pot is made of galvanised iron, as otherwise the undissolved crystals will destroy the surface of the pot. Care must be taken in weighing the ingredients, as too much tin can cause the wool to become harsh and brittle.

Iron (ferrous sulphate or copperas)
Iron is a very old mordant and is almost as important as alum. Great care has to be taken when using copperas to see that it is thoroughly dissolved and mixed with the water before the wool is entered, as otherwise there is danger of the wool's dyeing unevenly. The wool is also hardened if too much iron is used, or if it is boiled for too long. It is necessary to keep a separate utensil for mordanting and dyeing with iron, as the smallest trace of it will effect the brightness, iron being used mainly for darkening shades.

Iron can be used in the usual way for mordanting before dyeing, when the method of proceeding is as for mordanting with alum, and the recipe is as follows:

Recipe for mordanting 1 lb of wool
½ oz copperas
1 oz cream of tartar
It is, however, more generally the case with iron that the unmordanted wool is dyed first, and the copperas is added towards the end of the dyeing process. In this case the dye bath is brought slowly to the boil, and the wool is entered and left to simmer for one hour. Then the wool is removed, and the copperas and cream of tartar, having been thoroughly dissolved in water, are added to the dye bath and well stirred in before the wool is again entered and left to simmer for a further half hour. This process is known as 'saddening', probably because it has the effect of darkening the colour. Finally the wool after dyeing should be rinsed very thoroughly, if possible under running water, to keep it soft.

The principal natural dyestuffs
Cochineal, fustic, indigo, madder, flavine, cutch, logwood and weld are the principal imported natural materials for dyeing.

167

Red dyes

Cochineal (*coccus cacti*) is obtained from the dried bodies of a small scale-insect which feeds on the cactus plants cultivated for this purpose mainly in Mexico and the Canary Islands. There are two grades of cochineal, the silver and the black. One ounce of the top-grade black gives out more crimson dye than one ounce of the silver grade. It is more expensive than the silver grade, but, on the other hand, a smaller quantity is needed to produce the same amount of dye, and the colour obtained is more intense. A large range of colours is obtainable from cochineal, using different mordants: crimson with alum and cream of tartar; purples with chrome; scarlet with tin; silvery greys with iron.

Madder is derived from the ground-up, dried roots of a plant (*rubia tinctorum*) and is the best and most lasting red. It is Eurasian in origin and is one of the oldest dyes still used today. Hard water is recommended for use with this dye, and, if only soft water is available, a very little slaked lime (calcium hydroxide) should be added to the dye bath. This will help to brighten the colour. A gradual raising of the temperature of the dye bath is essential in order to bring out the maximum amount of colouring matter, but never boil for too long, as long boiling dulls and browns the colour. The dyeing utensil must be absolutely clean, and the wool must be washed well after mordanting and before dyeing, so as to get rid of all the surplus mordant. Some dyers add a handful of bran to a pound of wool when dyeing with madder in order to brighten the colour.

Yellow dyes

Weld (*reseda luteola*) is probably the oldest as it is the best yellow dye still in use and it is still cultivated in France, Germany and Italy for dyeing purposes. It takes longer to prepare than most of the other dye-stuffs, as the dried plants come in bundles, and, when it is needed for dyeing, the plants have to be broken into small pieces, using every part except the root. When used on wool, this dye imparts softness to the texture. It is the best and fastest natural yellow dye to use for silk dyeing.

Fustic There are two dye-producing plants known as fustic: *morus tinctoria*, the Dyers' Mulberry Tree or Old Fustic, which grows in the West Indies and Central America, and *cotinus coggyria* or Young Fustic, a large, ornamental shrub of Southern Europe and Asia, which is also known as Smoke Bush because the flowers form a grey, feathery head resembling a puff of smoke. Although this shrub is known as Young Fustic, it has been used as a dyewood for a much longer time than *morus tinctoria*. It is seldom used today, as *morus tinctoria*, which supplanted it, is much more permanent. The latter is sold in the form of yellowish chips.

Flavine or quercitron Flavine is the commercial name for a dye powder obtained from the inner bark of the oak tree, *quercus nigra* or *quercus tinctoria*, a native tree of the United States and Central America. Wool mordanted with tin and cream of tartar and dyed with flavine and cochineal produces a beautiful rich orange colour. Flavine is also much used for producing bright greens when used with indigo.

Brown dyes

Cutch (*catechu* or *acacia catechu*) is an old Indian dye obtained from the heartwood of various species of Acacia and Mimosa trees growing in

168

South-east Asia. Chips of this wood are boiled to make a gum resin which is the basis for a dye. It is particularly good for dyeing wool a rich brown colour and for shades of natural flesh colours. It is sold in dark brown lumps, which must be well pounded up before they can be used. Cutch should be stored in a dry place, as, once damp, it becomes very sticky and is difficult to pound.

Black and grey dyes

Logwood (*haematoxylin campeachianum*), a very useful dyewood from the east coast of Mexico and common in many parts of tropical America, is used for producing blacks, blues, greys and lavenders with different mordants. It is also very useful to employ with other dyes for the purpose of deepening the shades of a colour. Logwood is sold in the form of reddish chips, paste or liquid extract. When it was first introduced into this country, laws were passed prohibiting the use of it, as it was thought likely to bring discredit on the dyers by reason of the fugitiveness of the colours produced, but with proper mordants and with careful dyeing it can give good and fast colours. Used with a chrome mordant, logwood is the chief dyewood for making blacks. The chips should be boiled for half an hour just before the dye is used in order to extract it properly. It can be used for wool, cotton or silk.

Blue dyes

Indigo is the blue dye extracted from the plant *Indigofera tinctoria* which grows in South America, Asia and the Middle East. It is one of the ancient dye plants, a shrub of the legum family, and it is renowned for the clarity, beauty and fastness of the blue dye that it produces. The actual production of the dye depends on fermentation of the leaves, but most dyers buy indigo powder ready to use. This powder is insoluble in water, so a process different from the usual method of dyeing has to be adopted. There are two ways of doing this: in the first method the indigo powder is made into an extract by dissolving it in sulphuric acid or oil of vitriol, and in the second and more satisfactory method the indigo, hydrosulphite vat process is used. The first method results in a dye which gives a greenish-blue colour to wool, but it is not very permanent, and the dye cannot be used on cotton or linen. The second method produces beautiful fast colours and, although it is a more complicated process, it is quite within the powers of anyone to carry it out successfully, provided sufficient time and care are taken. It is, in fact, the only way to produce really fast blues and greens. The process involves depriving the indigo of its oxygen, for it is the deoxidised indigo, appearing yellow in colour whilst in the dye bath, which is able to penetrate into the woollen fibre, and the brightness and fastness of the blue obtained depends upon how well the vat has been deoxidised.

Recipes for dyeing

Crimson with cochineal
1 lb wool mordanted with alum and cream of tartar
2 oz cochineal for a good medium shade, with
½ oz logwood added, if a dark crimson is needed
1 dessertspoonful common salt.

METHOD

Add the cochineal and salt to a pot of warm water. There should be sufficient water comfortably to cover the wool. Stir well, increase the heat and put in the mordanted wool, gradually bringing the temperature up to boiling within half an hour. Reduce the heat and simmer gently just under boiling point for an hour or continue simmering until the required shade is obtained. If the wool is allowed to cool in the dye liquor, the colour will become a little deeper and more even. Remove the wool from the dye bath, wash it well, rinse thoroughly and dry in the shade. If, however, the required shade is reached quite early in the process, it may be necessary to weaken the dye bath. Remove the wool, empty part of the dye away, fill up the pot with extra water and continue dyeing. Even very pale shades must have the minimum of half an hour simmering, otherwise they will not be fast. It is better to dye with a weak solution for a longer time than with a strong solution for a shorter time. If a bright geranium red is required, this can be obtained by adding a few grains of oxalic acid crystals to the dye bath.

Crimson with cochineal and unmordanted wool
1 lb unmordanted wool
4 oz alum
$1\frac{1}{2}$ oz cream of tartar
$1\frac{1}{2}$–2 oz cochineal

METHOD

Dissolve the alum and cream of tartar in a little warm water and add to the dye pot containing sufficient warm water to cover the wool. Enter the washed and still damp wool, bring to the boil and simmer for half an hour. Remove the wool and add the cochineal to the pot. Stir well before re-entering the wool and continue simmering just under boiling point for a further hour. A slight addition of ammonia to the dye bath will make the shade bluer.

To dye a very small quantity of wool in a range of five shades of crimson with cochineal
$2\frac{1}{2}$–3 oz wool previously mordanted with alum and cream of tartar and divided into $\frac{1}{2}$ oz skeins
$\frac{1}{4}$–$\frac{1}{2}$ oz cochineal
   logwood
$\frac{1}{2}$ teaspoonful salt

METHOD

In this method a skein of wool at a time is removed from the dye bath, whilst the other skeins are re-entered and dyed for a further period of time to obtain darker shades.

Add $\frac{1}{4}$ oz cochineal and the salt to the dye pot and stir well. Slowly raise the temperature of the mixture and, when it is warm, put in the five skeins of wool. Bring to boiling point, turn down the heat and simmer gently. Divide the remaining $\frac{1}{4}$ oz cochineal into three equal parts. After half an hour remove all the wool and add one portion more of cochineal, stirring well before re-entering four of the skeins. Continue dyeing for another half an hour, then remove the wool once more from the pot and add another portion of cochineal. Repeat the process, returning only three skeins to the pot. After a further half an hour of simmering, remove the wool and add two to three small teaspoonfuls of logwood to give shade number four. Shade number five may require a small extra amount of both cochineal and logwood and slightly longer simmering to bring it to a really dark shade of crimson. After all the wool has been removed from the dye pot, the excessive liquid should be gently squeezed out of the wool. It is then washed and rinsed again and again, under running water if possible, until all surplus colour is removed. The wool is then hung in the shade to dry.

Purple with cochineal
Mordant with chrome, then wash and dye for one hour with 2 oz cochineal. This will give a good medium purple, and, if a darker shade is needed, a little logwood can be added half an hour before the end. A tablespoonful of vinegar added to the dye bath helps the colour. Wash thoroughly.

Mauve range : cochineal with chrome mordant and logwood
If the wool is mordanted with a chrome mordant instead of with alum and cream of tartar and is dyed with the same ingredients as those in the recipe for the crimson range, a range of mauve-purple shades will be obtained.

Soft mauve-grey range
1 lb unmordanted wool
½ oz iron
½ oz cream of tartar
2 oz cochineal

METHOD
Mordant the wool with iron and cream of tartar, then add the dye. If a range of shades is required, proceed as with the crimson range recipe.

Red with madder
1 lb wool mordanted with tin and cream of tartar
8 oz madder
A little precipitated chalk should be added, if the water is soft.

METHOD
Although it is not absolutely necessary, it is better to soak the madder dye overnight, as this makes it easier to use.

    Add the madder to the dye bath. Stir well, bring slowly to the boil and simmer just under boiling point for half an hour. Add a small amount more of water, if needed, and enter the wool. Simmer for an hour and allow the wool to cool in the dye bath. Then wash in several waters and pass through a boiling soap bath—in other words, put some soap powder in a vessel and enough water to cover the wool and boil hard for four minutes. This brightens and improves the colour.

Scarlet
1 lb wool mordanted with tin and cream of tartar
2 oz cochineal
1 tablespoonful salt

METHOD

Enter the wool into a cool dye bath and raise the temperature slowly to the boil. Simmer for one hour. Take out the wool, wash it and dry it in the shade.

Orange shade of scarlet with cochineal
1 lb wool mordanted with tin and cream of tartar
$\frac{1}{2}$ oz fustic, Persian berries or flavine
2 oz cochineal
1 tablespoonful common salt

METHOD

Put the 2 oz cochineal, the $\frac{1}{2}$ oz fustic and the salt into the dye bath, stirring well. When it has warmed up, enter the wool, bring it slowly to the boil and simmer for one hour. Take the wool out and wash it.

If the wool is too orange, boil it up in fresh, cold water, when it will become crimson. Dissolve a few tin crystals and a small quantity of oxalic acid crystals in water and add them, a little at a time, to the dye bath, stirring well each time before re-entering the wool, which must always be removed before a fresh amount of the solution is added.

Small quantity of wool to be dyed in a range of five shades of scarlet
5 oz unmordanted wool
$\frac{1}{4}$ oz tin crystals
$\frac{1}{4}$ oz oxalic acid crystals
$\frac{1}{2}$ oz cochineal, divided into five portions
3–4 teaspoonfuls of logwood

METHOD

Pound the tin, oxalic acid and one portion of cochineal in a mortar until quite fine and dissolve them in the dye bath, stirring thoroughly and remembering that no undissolved tin crystals must touch the wool, or they may rot it. Put in all the wool. There must be enough water in the pot to cover the five skeins of wool. Slowly bring to the boil and leave to simmer. After half an hour remove all of the wool and stir in another portion of cochineal. Return four of the skeins and continue dyeing for another half an hour. Continue like this, each time removing one skein of wool and adding another portion of cochineal in order to get the next skein a shade darker. Finally add the logwood, a portion at a time, for the last two shades. The method is the same as that given in the recipe for small quantities of wool to be dyed crimson with cochineal.

Lemon yellow
1 lb wool mordanted with alum and cream of tartar
2 oz fustic chips

METHOD

It is generally better to put the chips into a thin, roomy cotton bag to prevent their getting entangled in the wool. Put the bag into the bath of water together with the wool and bring to the boil during half an hour. Then simmer for a further half-hour.

The amount of fustic may be increased to 4 oz, if greater depth of colour is desired. The addition of 1 oz of flavine will make the colour a deeper and richer daffodil yellow.

Gold
1 lb of wool mordanted with chrome and dyed with 2 oz of fustic will give a gold colour, and, if 1 oz of madder is added, the colour will change to orange.

Reddish orange is obtained by mordanting 1 lb of wool with 4 oz of alum and 1 oz of cream of tartar, and dyeing with 4 oz of madder and 1 oz of fustic.

Orange
1 lb of wool mordanted with tin and cream of tartar
4 oz fustic or Persian berries
$\frac{1}{2}$ oz flavine
4 oz madder

METHOD
Boil the wool with the fustic and madder for half an hour. Remove the wool and add the flavine and simmer for three-quarters of an hour. Wash and dry the wool.

Daffodil yellow
1 lb of wool mordanted with chrome and cream of tartar
3 lb weld
$\frac{1}{2}$ oz precipitated chalk

METHOD
The weld should be cut up small and put into a pot of cold water with the dissolved chalk. Bring the temperature up to boiling point and let it simmer for an hour. Enter the wool and simmer for three-quarters of an hour. If preferred the weld may be tied loosely in a muslin bag. Wash and dry the wool.

Small quantity of wool to be dyed in a range of five shades of yellow with fustic or Persian berries (the five shades ranging from lemon through daffodil to olive, dark khaki and brown)
$2\frac{1}{2}$–3 oz wool previously mordanted with alum and cream of tartar and divided into $\frac{1}{2}$ oz skeins
$1\frac{1}{2}$ oz fustic chips
1 teaspoonful flavine
a few tin crystals
a few iron crystals
$\frac{1}{8}$ oz cutch
$\frac{1}{4}$–$\frac{1}{2}$ oz logwood

METHOD
Add 1 oz of the fustic chips to the water in the dye pot and simmer just below boiling point for half an hour. All of the wet wool should then be entered and simmered gently for three-quarters of an hour. Remove the wool from the pot and add the flavine and a few tin crystals, making sure the tin is thoroughly dissolved before adding it to the bath. Stir well and re-enter four skeins of wool. Simmer for half an hour, before removing the wool again and adding the remaining fustic. Dissolve a few iron

crystals in a little hot water and sadden the dye bath with a small quantity of this. Stir well, return three skeins to the pot and continue dyeing. Take out one skein after a quarter of an hour, if it is dark enough. At this stage a little more fustic or iron may be needed to darken the remaining skeins. Simmer for a further quarter to half an hour. To obtain the fifth and darkest shade to complete the range, remove the wool and add the cutch and logwood to the bath, replacing the last skein and continuing the dyeing until a rich brown is obtained. Rinse thoroughly in several waters and wash all the wool with soap flakes or Stergene. Hang out the wool to dry.

If 3 oz of wool are used, the odd extra skein of shade one can be kept in reserve in case two shades are dyed too near in colour to one another. If this happens, the spare skein can be dyed the correct shade to complete the range, the shades of which must be evenly spaced.

Medium grey
1 lb wool unmordanted
$\frac{1}{4}$ oz iron (copperas)
$\frac{1}{4}$ oz cutch

METHOD
Dissolve the cutch in the dye bath. Enter the wool, previously washed and left wet. Boil for 30 minutes. Remove the wool and put in the iron. Stir well and, when the iron is dissolved, bring the dye pot back to the boil. Re-enter the wool and continue boiling until the desired shade is obtained. Rinse under running water and wash.

To obtain a blue-grey shade more cutch and less iron is required.

Wool to be dyed in a range of three shades of grey
1 lb wool unmordanted and divided into three skeins
$\frac{1}{4}$ oz cutch
$\frac{1}{4}$ oz iron (copperas)

METHOD
Dissolve the cutch in the dye bath and bring slowly to the boil. Enter the well-washed and still wet wool and simmer. After 30 minutes remove one skein and continue dyeing for a further 30 minutes. Remove the second skein and leave the third to simmer for another 30 minutes. Dissolve the iron in a little hot water. Transfer the cutch dye liquid to the saucepan kept solely for iron mordant; add the iron mordant; stir thoroughly and bring to the boil. Re-enter the three skeins of wool and, when the desired shades have been obtained, remove the wool once more. Rinse thoroughly in warm water.

Fawn

To dye a small quantity of wool in a range of three shades of fawn the above recipe for grey should be used, but using $\frac{1}{8}$ oz cutch instead of $\frac{1}{4}$ oz.

Soft mahogany-brown colour with cutch
1 lb wool mordanted with alum and cream of tartar
$\frac{1}{4}$ oz–$\frac{1}{2}$ oz cutch

METHOD

Dissolve the cutch in the dye bath and boil gently for 30 minutes or until the desired shade is obtained. Rinse immediately in plenty of warm water several times.

Brown

1 lb wool mordanted with iron and cream of tartar or unmordanted
8 oz madder
Add a little precipitated chalk, if the water is soft, as madder dyes better in hard water.

METHOD

For mordanted wool see the recipe for red with madder.

For unmordanted wool dye the wool first for half an hour with the madder. Remove the wool and add the well-dissolved iron and cream of tartar to the dye bath. Stir well and re-enter the wool and continue dyeing for another half an hour.

Black

1 lb wool mordanted with $\frac{1}{2}$ oz chrome
8 oz logwood

METHOD

Put the logwood into the dye bath and boil for half an hour. Then enter the wool and continue boiling for at least an hour. Remove the wool from the dye pot and wash thoroughly, rinsing well under running water if possible. Add a teaspoonful of sulphuric acid to the washing water. This will help to fix the colour and prevent rubbing. If sulphuric acid is used, always add the acid with great care drop by drop to the water and never add water to the acid, because, if this is done, it generates great heat and causes the acid to erupt violently, when it will burn anything it touches. Always have handy some liquid ammonia when using sulphuric acid. This, if applied at once, will neutralise the burning action of the acid, if any should get on hands or clothes. Water is useless for this purpose.

The above recipe will give a blue-black colour. For a dead black add $\frac{1}{2}$ oz of fustic chips to the mordant bath. For a brown-black shade add cutch or walnut to the mordant.

Blue

Indigo vat. Hydro-sulphite vat process sufficient to dye 8 oz wool
$1\frac{1}{2}$ oz caustic soda
1 oz hydro-sulphite soda. This must be very fresh with no lumps
1 oz powdered indigo
1 stone jar with lid, or an empty wine or beer bottle with cork. This is to hold the stock solution. Any stock solution left over will keep for a certain length of time, provided it is kept from the light.
1 jug containing hot water at a temperature of 49–54 °C (120–130 °F)
2 jugs to hold about $\frac{1}{2}$ pint each
1 enamelled saucepan (aluminium must not be used)
1 glass or plastic mixing rod
1 water thermometer

METHOD

Put 1 oz of powdered indigo into a mortar, add the smallest amount of warm water and grind the indigo with a pestle into a liquid paste. Put the paste into the saucepan.

Put $\frac{1}{2}$ pint of hot water into one of the jugs and gradually enter the caustic soda, stirring with the rod the whole time. Take the other jug with $\frac{1}{2}$ pint of hot water and gradually add the hydro-sulphite soda, stirring with the rod. First add to the indigo nearly all of the caustic soda solution and then nearly all of the hydro-sulphite solution. Stir and warm up gradually to 52 °C (125 °F) and leave for half an hour off the heat, but in a warm place. From this point on great care must be taken with the temperature, and the thermometer must be in use all the time from now until the end of the dyeing process. If the temperature goes beyond 60 °C (140 °F), the whole vat is ruined, and the process has to be started all over again.

After half an hour it is necessary to test the solution by using the glass rod. When the latter is dipped into the solution and then removed again, the liquid remaining on it should show a perfectly clear yellow colour free from spots. This yellow colour should turn to blue in approximately 45 seconds. If dark spots are to be seen in the liquid, this means that some of the indigo is undissolved, and, in this case, 2–2½ tablespoonfuls of the hydro-sulphite solution should be gradually added to the indigo solution. Wait 15 minutes and test again. If the solution is still incorrect, continue adding similar amounts of hydro-sulphite every 15 minutes until the glass rod indicates clear yellow.

If the stock solution is greenish-white and turbid, this indicates that indigo white is present, and that too much hydro-sulphite was used. Add rather less than half a teaspoonful at a time of caustic soda solution. Stir gently until the stock solution is corrected and answers to the glass rod test.

To dye with indigo vat 5 oz wool. To dye a range of five shades
Fill a vessel with water and bring the temperature up to hand-hot (52 °C and not higher than 60 °C). Before one can dye with indigo, it has to be deprived of its oxygen. To do this add 2½ fluid oz of hydro-sulphite solution ($\frac{1}{4}$ oz hydro-sulphite to $\frac{1}{8}$ pint of water = 2½ oz hydro-sulphite solution) and 1 oz salt. Stir well and leave for 20 minutes, and this will deoxygenate the water. Then add one tablespoonful of the indigo stock solution. Stir very gently without making bubbles. The bath should appear greenish yellow and should not feel slimy as this indicates too much caustic soda, and some more hydro-sulphite solution must be added. The surface of the liquid in the vat may appear iridescent, but underneath it should be quite clear. The vat is now ready to dye.

The damp skeins of wool should be gathered up tightly with both hands and, still tightly held, they should be very carefully slipped into the dye without causing any bubbles. Keeping the hands still under the surface of the liquid, carefully spread the wool over the bottom of the pot and then, just as carefully, withdraw the hands. On no account shake the liquid off the hands so that it falls back into the bath, as this will only carry air back into the liquid. It is better to have an old cloth near at hand to receive the drips.

After half an hour in the dye, the wool should be removed in the same way as it was entered, by slipping both hands under the dye and gathering up the wool, squeezing it hard once or twice under the surface and, whilst still squeezing it, gently bringing it out. Quickly squeeze—not wring—the excess liquid out. Shake each individual skein and at the same time keep it moving around so that no surplus moisture is allowed to settle in any one spot. Separate, as far as possible each strand of wool in order for the air to circulate. It is only on exposure to the air that the colour of the wool will change to blue.

Now hang out the wool in the air for half an hour, after which time, if the shade of blue is correct, it must be returned to the dye bath for a further half an hour, without the addition of any more stock solution. This process must be repeated at least three times in order to make the colour permanent: the wool must be in the bath for half an hour and out for the same length of time. The greater the number of dippings in the dye and hangings out in the air, the greater the permanence of the colour.

After the lightest shade has been obtained, before returning the rest of the wool, add another tablespoonful of the stock solution to the bath and repeat the process, adding extra stock solution each time a darker shade is required. It makes for greater fastness of colour to build up a good, deep shade by a series of dips in a weak vat, than to use one or two very strong baths. If there is difficulty in obtaining a really dark blue, a little logwood can be added to the last shade.

When the dyeing is finished, the wool should be washed at least twice. A teaspoonful of sulphuric acid is sometimes added to the first water to neutralise the caustic soda used. Finally the wool should be put through a boiling soap bath. The water and soap flakes should be brought to the boil and the wool entered and boiled hard for four minutes. This will help to clear any surplus dye and prevent the colour from rubbing. Rinse well.

If after all this has been done, the colour should rub off badly, try washing the wool in Fuller's earth, and, if the shade is then too pale, re-dye the wool. If the vat has been badly managed, the wool may be dull. In this case, pass the wool through a hot bath of 99 per cent water and 1 per cent acetic acid, wash twice in soap and water and rinse well. If the wool is streaky, take two gallons of water at 49 °C (120 °F) with $\frac{1}{4}$ oz hydro-sulphite powder and one tablespoonful of liquid ammonia (fort. 880), put the wool into it and let it stay there for one hour. Wash it in two waters, rinse and dry.

If the vat turns blue during the process of dyeing, it may be the result of incorrect preparation, or it may be because, through bad management in the process, such as causing bubbles or allowing drops of the liquid to fall from the hands into the bath whilst entering the wool, air has been reintroduced into the deoxygenised vat. In this case add 2–3 fluid oz of hydro-sulphite solution, bring the temperature up to 54 °C (130 °F) and leave it for 30 minutes.

Green
There is no satisfactory dye plant which will supply a green colour, so the wool must first be dyed blue and then overdyed with yellow. To obtain a blue-green, first mordant the blue-dyed wool with alum and cream of tartar and then dye with a weak solution of fustic or weld. To obtain a bright green, dye the white wool to a medium shade of blue, then mordant

with tin and cream of tartar and dye with 1 oz of fustic or weld. To green a range of blue wool, mordant the whole range with tin and cream of tartar and enter all the wool into a dye bath of fustic, weld or Persian berries. This will not alter the range of shades at all; it will only change the colour.

252
253

254

255

252–5   Vegetable dyeing

252   One method of tying the wool before washing

253   A method of tying skeins of wool for dyeing when the skeins have been cut

254   After being washed in soap and water, the wool must be rinsed thoroughly and the strands of wool must be separated as far as possible in order to allow the dye to penetrate the fibres evenly

255   A range of vegetable-dyed wool. There must be a definite but not too violent break between the shades in a range of colour

256

257

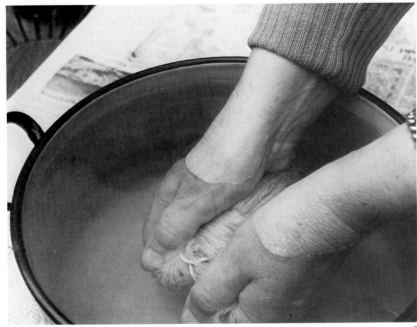

256–8 Dyeing with indigo

258

256 Entering the wool carefully into the dye bath to avoid making bubbles. This prevents air from being taken into the bath

257 The thermometer shows the temperature in the dye bath coming up to 54 °C (130 °F)

258 Before the wool is removed from the dye bath it is squeezed once or twice very firmly but gently

Suppliers of natural dyestuffs and mordants

L. A. HORNER AND SONS LIMITED
9 Colworth Grove
London, SE17

COMAK CHEMICALS LIMITED
Department MCG/P, Swinton Works
Moon Street
London, N1

7 Mounting finished work

When the work is finished and taken off the frame, it generally needs pulling back into shape. This is particularly the case with pieces of work in which tent stitch and other diagonal stitches have been considerably used, as these stitches tend to pull the canvas out of shape much more than do the square stitches.

To stretch a finished piece of work lay it face downwards upon a drawing-board which has first been covered with clean white paper or white cotton material. It is better not to use brown paper for this purpose, as this may stain the work. When stretching a square or rectangular panel, start with one side straight along the edge of the drawing-board, stretch it to its uttermost and pin it out along the edge of the board with drawing-pins, putting the pins into the unworked canvas at about 1 in. intervals. Now stretch one of the other sides at right angles to the first side and, having got it into position, pin down the corner first and then work back, pinning this side down at intervals in the same way as the first. The position for the other sides of the square or rectangle should now be drawn in on the paper or material covering the drawing-board, and the piece of work should be stretched and pulled so that the fourth corner can be pinned down in the position drawn for it on the board. Finally the two unpinned sides should be stretched to fit on to the rectangular shape on the board and should be pinned down as were the other sides. In order to make the stretching of these two sides possible, some water may be sprinkled over the back surface of the work and rubbed well into the canvas, but avoiding all areas worked with silk, as water penetrates more quickly through silk than wool, and it may stain the front of the work with colouring from the canvas thread. When the work is pinned down securely all round, it should be left for 24 hours to dry thoroughly and to complete the stretching process. On removal from the board, it should have returned to its original shape.

If a canvas has been worked throughout with double wool and is difficult to stretch, it may be necessary to use tintacks instead of drawing-pins for fixing the work down on the board, and it may also be necessary to put these tacks into the actual worked part of the canvas in order to avoid tearing the canvas as a result of the extra strain which occurs when stretching such heavy pieces of work. Putting the tacks into the worked part of the canvas should not cause any damage, provided they are placed carefully into the holes left between stitches and are not left in position for too long. To stretch such heavier pieces of work a pair of upholsterer's stretchers may also prove helpful.

When the work to be stretched is not rectangular in shape, the template must first be drawn on to the paper covering the drawing-board, and the worked canvas should then be placed upon it and stretched to fit it as exactly as possible.

To mount a panel of canvas work it is necessary to obtain a piece of hardboard or plywood exactly the same shape and size as the worked part of the canvas. The panel is then stretched firmly upon this backing. Generally it is better to glue the edges of the surplus canvas all round the panel to the back of the board in order to maintain a good even tension on the front surface of the work. The method of lacing across the back of the panel with strong thread can be used on very small pieces of work, but it is not suitable for large panels where the tension is very great.

If it is at all possible, it is better to carry out this mounting yourself, in order to ensure that the work is mounted absolutely square and without puckers. Some picture-framers will undertake to do the mounting as well, but it should always be made clear to them beforehand what are the special requirements in mounting canvas work satisfactorily. Framing is a matter of taste, but it should be remembered that canvas embroideries are better hung unglazed.

To mount canvas-work chair seats and stool tops it is generally more satisfactory to take them to a professional upholsterer, who can make any necessary adjustments to the stuffing.

For mounting mirror surrounds bevelled or unbevelled mirror glass may be used. If bevelled glass is used, it should be placed in the centre of a backboard of $\frac{1}{2}$ in. thick hardboard or plywood. The backboard must then be built up slightly all round the mirror to the thickness of the glass by glueing pieces of hardboard, plywood or card upon it. This will hold the glass in the required position. Then the worked surround is mounted on some material which will not warp, such as thin hardboard or plywood, cut to the exact size of the surround. It needs to be remembered that the mirror glass must be slightly larger than the aperture in the surround. The latter is then glued carefully into position, and the mirror should be held quite firmly by it. Finally the whole thing is suitably framed.

If unbevelled glass is used, the easiest way is to cut the glass the same size as the hardboard base, upon which it is fixed with mirror clips. Then place the mounted mirror surround in place upon the glass and frame the whole.

Figure 263 shows a more unusual mirror surround. It is designed with 2 in. polystyrene cubes covered with needlework, which are mounted upon a 24 in. square unbevelled mirror backed with plywood and fastened at the corners with mirror clips. Four cubes along each side are joined together with bars of canvas, which are worked with Smyrna, cross and tent stitches, as is also the outside edge which covers the edges of the backboard and the mirror. The cubes are fixed to the mirror with a strong glue.

When a heavy plate glass is used for mirrors, it gives a deep reflection, so all work placed on the surface of the glass must be lined in some way. For instance, when a surround is mounted on board, the cut edge of the canvas, which has to be stuck down on the underneath of the mounting-board, must be oversewn with the background wool, or extra rows of stitching can be worked before the centre aperture is cut out of the canvas, and these will mask the thickness of the mounting-board when stuck down, and prevent any unworked canvas being reflected. The cubes used on the mirror shown in figure 263 were lined with gold leather.

259   One of a pair of wedding stools. The completed canvas before mounting is shown here. It was worked in ranges of yellow and grey wool with silk highlights on a white wool background in cushion stitch on 16-mesh canvas

Lilian Hill for St Luke's Church, Eltham Park, SE9

260   Lamp base partly worked with gold leather and black PVC together with Smyrna stitch and cross stitch in wool and goldfingering knitting yarn

261   Table lamp base being stretched before making up

262   The same two table lamp bases mounted   *Lilian Hill*

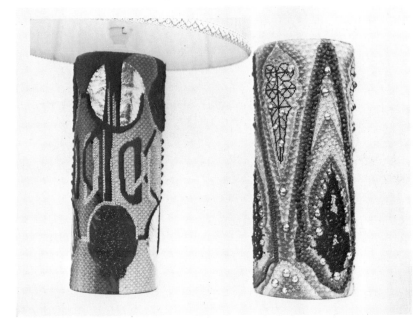

263　Mirror surround mounted on the mirror

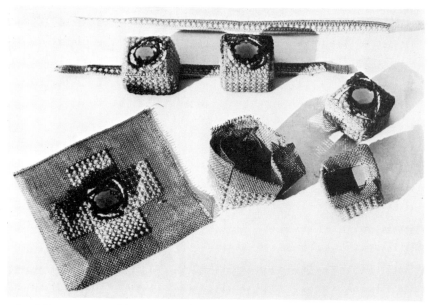

264　Mirror surround in process of being assembled. Box shapes linked together form the surround. The cubes are filled with blocks of polystyrene. Topaz and amethyst jewels are used here with Smyrna stitch in shades of purple and yellow

Lilian Hill

265 Three-dimensional cross. The cross is worked mainly in white perlé, wool and silk. Diamond shapes were cut out of the canvas, and pieces of yellow-green antique stained glass in various shades have been placed behind. The small black crosses on the glass are formed by taking three or four threads across the hole and weaving over and under these threads   *Lilian Hill*

266 Mounting the cross. The worked canvas has here been mounted on hardboard, and the picture shows the holes cut in the canvas and the bars worked across them before the glass has been placed into position. The canvas is cut away to within an inch of the worked part all round. It is then turned under and stuck down. The finished cross is mounted on 1 in. high wooden blocks which have been covered with canvas worked with stitchery. The cross is then fixed to the background with screws

267 Evening bag (front). Metal thread and small pearls were used on a filoselle silk tent-stitch background
Winnie Browning

Conclusion

I have attempted in writing this book to approach the subject in a way which, I hope, will encourage the newcomer to canvas work to take pleasure in the creation of designs of her own, instead of resorting to the usual commercial traced canvases or adhering to the preconceived idea that all canvas work must necessarily be based on geometric patterns. I have also tried to show how different textures can be obtained, not only by using a variety of stitches, but also by using different shades of colour with one type of stitch. The reader may have noticed that very few sketches of actual stitches have been included in this book. This omission is entirely intentional, as it seemed unnecessary to include very many of them, when so many books have been published in recent years giving full coverage of stitches. I have, however, shown in diagrams how the main stitches are worked and have supported these diagrams with many close-up photographs in an endeavour to demonstrate clearly how stitches can best be used. I consider that the knowledge of how stitches are best used in conjunction with one another to interpret a design is much more important than the simple knowledge of how to work individual stitches. If any reader has found sufficient interest in these methods of working to be encouraged to try out other interesting ways of working on canvas, which will once again help to popularise and raise the standard of this old craft, then my work will have served its purpose.

Suppliers of materials and equipment

Great Britain

Canvas, Appleton's crewel and tapestry wools, twisted embroidery silks, Maltese silk and all embroidery accessories

Mrs Mary Allen
Wirksworth, Derbyshire DE4 4BN

The Royal School of Needlework
25 Princes Gate
South Kensington, London, SW7

Art Needlework Industries Ltd
7 St Michael's Mansions
Ship Street, Oxford

Canvas and wools and all other embroidery accessories

Harrods Ltd
Brompton Road, London, SW1

Winchester canvas, linen substitute, silk cords, coton a broder and all embroidery equipment, including metal threads and orion cloth

Handworkers' Market
6 Bull Street
Holt, Norfolk NR25 6HP

Mace and Nairn
89 Crane Street
Salisbury, Wiltshire

Christine Riley
53 Barclay Road
Stonehaven, Kincardineshire,
Scotland AB3 2AR

Wools, silks, frames, needles and all accessories

I. M. Jervie
21/23 West Port
Arbroath, Angus, Scotland

Felt and hessian

The Felt and Hessian Shop
34 Greville Street, London, EC1

Winchester canvas linen substitute, Appletons, crewel and tapestry wools and all embroidery equipment

Mrs Joan L. Trickett
110 Marsden Road
Burnley, Lancashire

Atherstone wool, raffene and a good variety of weaving yarns, frames and needles

Dryad Ltd
Northgates, Leicester

100 per cent pure two-ply wool

Tulloch of Shetland Ltd
Lerwick, Scotland

DMC threads perlé, tapestry and crewel wools

de Denne Limited
159/161 Kenton Road
Kenton
Harrow, Middlesex HA3 0EU

M. R. Ltd
1a Thornford Road
Lewisham, London, SE13

DMC and Lurex threads

Bernina Service
3 Burton's Arcade
Leeds 1, Yorkshire

Crewel and tapestry wools

Appleton Brothers of London
Church Street, Chiswick, London
W4

Metal threads

Benton and Johnston Ltd
63 King's Cross Road, London WC1
(Postal orders only)

Toye Kenning and Spencer Ltd
Regalia House
26 Red Lion Square, London WC1

Coloured and tissue papers

Paperchase Limited
213 Tottenham Court Road,
London W1

Stained glass

Goddard and Gibbs
49 Kingsland Road, London, E2

'Shisha' glass

Maharani Ltd
10 Quadrant Arcade
80–82 Regent Street, London, W1

Jewels, beads and sequins

Ells and Farrier
5 Princes Street, London, W1

The Bead Shop
53 South Molton Street, London,
W1

Picture framers

Ernest Wheatley
45 Maddox Street, London, W1

USA

Crewel and tapestry wool

Appleton Brothers of London
West Main Road
Little Compton
Rhode Island 02837

Appleton's wools, silk floss

American Crewel Studio
Box 298, Boonton
New Jersey 07005

Canvas, wools and accessories

Bucky King
Embroideries Unlimited
Box 371, King Bros
3 Ranch Buffalo Star Rte
Sheriden
Wyoming 82801

American Thread Corporation
90 Park Avenue, New York

Index

The numbers in *italic* refer to illustrations